Risking a New Beginning

Jack Cabaness

Parson's Porch
Book Publishing

Risking a New Beginning

ISBN: Softcover 978-1-946478-48-1

Copyright © 2017 by Jack Cabaness

All rights reserved. No part of this book may be reproduced or transmitted in any form or by any means, electronic or mechanical, including photocopying, recording, or by any information storage and retrieval system, without permission in writing from the publisher.

All scripture quotations are from the New Revised Standard Version.

To order additional copies of this book, contact:

Parson's Porch Books
1-423-475-7308
www.parsonsporch.com

Parson's Porch Books is an imprint of **Parson's Porch & Book Publishers** in Cleveland, Tennessee, which has double focus. We focus on the needs of creative writers who need a professional publisher to get their work to market, **&** we also focus on the needs of others by sharing our profits with those who struggle in poverty to meet their basic needs of food, clothing, shelter and safety.

Risking a New Beginning

Contents

First Things—In Search of Community
Riding to Church Barefoot on a Bike 11

Sermons on Parables
What Not to Wear to the Cedarcrest Prom 21
The Gospel According to Birth Order 29
Your Fair Share of the Rain 38
Don't Ask Me What It Means. I Don't Know. 48

Sermons on the Book of Job
Have You Considered My Servant Job? 61
The Patience of Job 66
Behemoth in a Hamster Wheel 74
Risking a New Beginning 82

Sermons Rewritten on Saturday in Response to Friday's News
Why Did Jesus Have to Die? 93
Working Through the Unimaginable 102

Last Things—Sermons on Ultimate Hopes
Judgment Day 113
From Dust to Life 122

A Note to the Reader

I find it hard to believe that I'm able to assemble a collection of sermons that spans twenty years—from 1996 to 2016. This collection includes sermons from my seminary intern year in California, as well as from churches I've pastored in Vermont, Colorado, and New York. There are sermons on the Parables of Jesus, on the Book of Job, and sermons that wrestle with current events, including two sermons that were substantially rewritten on Saturday in response to the news on Friday.

I once heard it said that preaching on the Parables of Jesus was "a young preacher's dream and an older preacher's nightmare." In this collection you'll find sermons on Jesus' parables from a young preacher and from an older one. I do know that in my early years I was eager to tackle the hardest parables, such as the "Unjust Steward" or "Dishonest Manager" of Luke 16:1-8, and now I approach the parables with considerably greater caution.

In this collection you'll find four sermons preached on the Book of Job, which is a task that I approached with tremendous humility and caution. I'm in debt to Samuel Balentine's commentary on the Book of Job, and to Thomas G. Long's book *What Shall We Say? Evil, Suffering, and the Crisis of Faith* for immensely helpful insights into Job.

During the 2015-2016 program year the Katonah Presbyterian Church committed to reading through Brian McLaren's book *We Make the Road by Walking*. We had small group discussions of the book, and each week the sermon was in dialogue with the scripture texts and the pertinent chapter in McLaren's book. You'll find two of those sermons in this collection: "Working Through the Unimaginable" and "Judgment Day."

This collection does not contain any sermons preached in Kansas City when I was an associate pastor, which was a time when I was trying to preach without the use of notes, and the full manuscripts were either not written or not preserved and any surviving notes resemble long-forgotten shopping lists. However, I believe that echoes from those Kansas City sermons can still be heard in the future sermons, and I am extremely grateful for the encouragement as well as honest dialogue about the sermons from many Kansas City friends and from friends in each of the congregations I have been privileged to serve as a pastor.

Finally, this collection is dedicated to my wife Emma, whose encouragement and honest dialogue have helped me grow as a preacher, and more importantly, as a husband and as a Christian.

Jack Cabaness
Katonah, New York
September 5, 2017

First Things—In Search of Community

Riding to Church Barefoot on a Bike
Katonah Presbyterian Church
Katonah, New York
April 17, 2016

So those who welcomed [Peter's] message were baptized, and that day about three thousand persons were added. They devoted themselves to the apostles' teaching and fellowship, to the breaking of bread and the prayers. Awe came upon everyone, because many signs and wonders were being done by the apostles. All who believed were together and had all things in common; They would sell their possessions and goods and distribute the proceeds to all, as any had need. Day by day, as they spent much time together in the temple, they broke bread at home and ate their food with glad and generous hearts, praising God and having the goodwill of all the people. And day by day the Lord added to their number those who were being saved.—Acts 2:41-47

One Sunday after worship, when Emma and I were still living in Colorado, I was scrolling through my Facebook feed, and I found a post by a well-known Christian blogger named Rachel Held Evans. What she wrote immediately captivated my attention. She wrote: "For all the people who come home from church feeling lonelier than when they left, please know you are not alone today."

Within 48 hours, that post generated 187 comments and 1,872 likes. Now, this was before Facebook launched their full range of emotional responses, so a "Like" certainly did not imply that people liked what she said, only that she had struck a nerve!

The first person who commented wrote, "that happens to me every time."

I continued to scroll through the posts. Some of the posts were written by people who said that they had stopped going to church and wondered why no one (including the pastor) had ever called them.

Some of the posts were written by pastors who said that they, too, sometimes felt lonelier after worship than before.

One person described how during the Passing of the Peace, the people around her shook hands first with the people they had known for years, and if someone did manage to shake her hand, it seemed more like an afterthought.

One person dogmatically asserted that people who truly know Jesus shouldn't be lonely.

And the very next comment was, "Why thank you, Preachy McPreachy, for thoroughly dismissing everyone's feelings. What you said would be like telling a hungry child that 'you're praying that they'll find a meal soon' instead of giving them one yourself. Don't pray for me. Talk to Me. I think that's what most folks here are saying."

That last post reminded me of a conversation I had with a father of three young children, who were part of the church in Colorado. Over time the family participated in worship less and less. He said, "Every time we come, people tend to say, 'You have a beautiful family,' but the conversation never goes deeper than that."

Perhaps the reason that Rachel's post struck such a nerve is that many people come to worship hoping to make connections, and they feel lonelier when it doesn't happen. People may also be struck by the difference between the way that they actually experience church and the way that the church is described in the second chapter of Acts.

According to Luke, who wrote the Acts of the Apostles, "Awe came upon everyone. All who believed were together and had all things in common. Day by day, as they spent much time together in the temple, they broke bread at home and ate their food with glad and generous hearts, praising God and having the goodwill of all the people. And day by day the Lord added to their number those who were being saved."

It does sound a little *daunting*, doesn't it? Awe came upon *everyone!* *All* who believed were together and had *all* things in common.

How on earth are we in today's church supposed to live up to *that?*

The good news is that it's not up to us alone. Luke's theology is truly in high gear at this point. Luke wants us to look beyond the individual apostles and believers and to see for ourselves how the prime mover in all of this is the Holy Spirit, the one who, as our own Presbyterian Brief Statement of Faith puts it, "binds us together with all believers in the one body of Christ, the Church."

Can we see, even in the messiness of our church life together, how the Holy Spirit is slowly but surely binding us together? Can we see why striving to be connected is essential, even when we might be tempted to give up on church and become spiritual lone rangers?

Church historian Martin Marty, who retired from the University of Chicago, has been an observer of American Christianity for well over sixty years. He believes that even in an age when many claim to be spiritual but not religious, that people still find that they have to bond together. He writes, "I once saw a bumper sticker that said, 'Spirituality doesn't make hospice calls.' Spirituality remains, normally, individualistic. You may gather for a retreat, and then you disperse. The people who are working with the homeless and dealing with addiction and trying to improve senior care and who care about the training of the young—they have to bond together. If they don't do it in old-fashioned churches, they'll do it in new-fashioned churches."[1]

Somebody once said that in the case of Christianity, it's a very material faith because you can't even get it going without a loaf of bread and a bottle of wine.[2]

---

[1] Interview of Martin Marty by Bob Abernathy, Religion and Ethics Newsweekly, May 3, 2002.

[2] Ibid.

As Luke puts it, the believers devoted themselves to the apostles' teaching and fellowship, to the breaking of bread and the prayers.

And as Jesus put it, "Where two or three are gathered together in my name, there I am also." That's a fairly familiar quotation. We preachers are apt to quote it to console ourselves when only two or three people show up for the Bible Study. But do you remember where in the Gospels Jesus said, "where two or three are gathered together in my name, there I am also?" It was in Matthew 18, where Jesus was talking honestly about church conflict. Jesus promises to be with us as we sort through the messiness of our church life together.

Living into a vision of a church where the Lord is always adding to our number isn't easy. Even the best churches can be cliquish. They have their share of bullies and wounded souls and very well-meaning people who simply assume that because they personally have felt welcomed in their own church that everyone else must feel included, too.

To live up to the vision presented in Acts requires the willingness to ask tough questions about how people really experience our churches.

What really happens during our coffee hour? Do we reach out to newcomers, or do we first have a tendency to talk to our friends that we've known for years?

The more we can engage each other in authentic, truth-telling conversation, then the more we can learn how to transcend the limits of our hospitality. And the more we can learn from each other as well.

A few years ago, the hospitality of the church we served in Colorado was stretched in an unexpected and delightful way. One Sunday morning two ten-year-old girls, Anna and Shyla, rode their bikes barefoot to church, unaccompanied by parents or by any other family members. They simply showed up. Shyla explained to me that they were sisters, and should I be confused by the fact that they were the same age, I should take into account that they were really half-sisters, with different mothers but the same dad. And then Shyla said that I could always remember that her name was Shyla because she was so shy, and Anna burst out laughing.

I loved that—a ten-year-old girl with a beautiful sense of irony, confidently and assertively telling me that she was shy.

Anna and Shyla told me that their moms had to work on Sunday mornings, so I went to their home during the week to get a permission form signed so that they could participate in youth group activities and come to worship by themselves. I visited a little with Anna's mom and learned that they weren't sisters at all, but friends and next-door neighbors who liked to pretend that they were sisters, but the part about their mothers having to work on Sunday mornings turned out to be true.

When Anna and Shyla returned to worship the next Sunday, they weren't barefoot anymore; they were wearing roller blades. They very nearly ran over 90-year-old Geraldine, but

Geraldine, who had never had any children of her own and who had taught Sunday School for over 50 years, simply told the girls that they were always welcome to sit with her whenever they came to church.

The following Sunday Anna came back to worship and she brought her pet mouse. The mouse was not in any kind of box or carrier, Anna just carried it with her in her shirt sleeve. For a while there, each Sunday presented a new and delightful challenge.

This congregation has its own encouraging stories to tell. Twice in the last year we've had parents writing letters to this congregation about their transgender children. And I'm grateful that those letters were shared, because otherwise it could be too easy to assume that of course, we're a progressive and welcoming and open congregation, and we don't need to be educated about someone else's journey. But we do need to be educated, and we need to take the time to listen and try to understand. And we have been trying to do just that. The parents in both families have repeatedly shared how overwhelmed and touched they have been by your letters of support. It's an ongoing journey, and there is much to learn and keep learning for all of us.

As a church may we keep learning what it means to include someone we've watched grow up and thought we knew, and may we also be ready to welcome the child who rides to church barefoot on a bike.

Sermons on Parables

What Not to Wear to the Cedarcrest Prom

Katonah Presbyterian Church
Katonah, New York
October 12, 2014

Then Jesus said to him, "Someone gave a great dinner and invited many. At the time for the dinner he sent his slave to say to those who had been invited, 'Come; for everything is ready now.' But they all alike began to make excuses. The first said to him, 'I have bought a piece of land, and I must go out and see it; please accept my regrets.' Another said, 'I have bought five yokes of oxen, and I am going to try them out; please accept my regrets.' Another said, 'I have just been married, and therefore I cannot come.' So the slave returned and reported this to his master. Then the owner of the house became angry and said to his slave, 'Go out at once into the streets and lanes of the town and bring in the poor, the crippled, the blind, and the lame.' And the slave said, 'Sir, what you ordered has been done, and there is still room.' Then the master said to the slave, 'Go out into the roads and lanes, and compel people to come in, so that my house may be filled. For I tell you, none of those who were invited will taste my dinner.'"

—Luke 14:16-24

Once more Jesus spoke to them in parables, saying: "The kingdom of heaven may be compared to a king who gave a wedding banquet for his son. He sent his slaves to call those who had been invited to the wedding banquet, but they would not come. Again, he sent other slaves, saying, 'Tell those who have been invited: Look, I have prepared my dinner, my oxen and my fat calves have been slaughtered, and everything is ready; come to the wedding banquet.' But they made light of it and went away, one to his farm, another to his business, while the rest seized his slaves, mistreated them, and killed them. The king was enraged. He sent his troops, destroyed those murderers, and burned their city. Then he said to his slaves, 'The wedding is ready, but those invited were not worthy. Go therefore into the main streets, and invite everyone you find to the wedding banquet.' Those slaves went out into the streets and gathered all whom they found, both good and bad; so, the wedding hall was filled with guests. "But when the king came in to see the guests, he noticed a man there who was not wearing a wedding robe, and he said to him, 'Friend, how did you get in here without a wedding robe?' And he was speechless. Then the king said to the attendants, 'Bind him hand and foot, and throw him into the outer darkness, where there will be weeping and gnashing of teeth.' For many are called, but few are chosen."

—Matthew 22:1-14

Now that's a very different version of the parable from the one that we heard in Luke! In Luke's version, someone gives a great dinner, but all the invited guests have excuses for why they can't come. The house owner then tells his servant to go out into the streets and lanes of the town and bring in the poor, the crippled, the blind, and the lame. The servant reports back that what the house owner had ordered was done and that there is still more room at the banquet. So the house owner told him to go out into the roads and lanes and compel people to come, so that the house would be full. Finally, the house owner, with a seemingly surly reply, declares that none of the original invited guests will taste the dinner. That's Luke's version of the parable.

In Matthew's version of the parable people actually die. A king gives a wedding banquet for his son. When the king's slaves go out to spread the word, some of them are mistreated and killed. Then the king sent his troops to destroy the murderers and burn their city. Somehow a spurned banquet invitation led to all-out war. I prefer Luke's version of the parable, where the house owner simply says to the no-shows, "Well, no dinner for you!"

We shake our heads at the gratuitous violence in Matthew's parable, but the original hearers of the gospel would have heard references to recent events. Remember that the Gospel writer Matthew is retelling Jesus' parable for the members of Matthew's church, who probably lived in Syria between the years 80 and 90. To them the reference to the destroyed city would have been heard as a reference to the Fall of Jerusalem in AD 70. The earlier mistreatment and murder of the slaves would have been heard as a reference to Israel's rejection of the prophets. And the members of Matthew's church would have likely recognized themselves as the last-minute replacement wedding guests assembled in the great wedding hall.[3]

What happens next is that the king arrives in the banquet hall to see the guests, and he notices that one guest in particular is not wearing a wedding robe. The king says, "Friend, how did you get in here without a wedding robe?"

This is another difference between Luke and Matthew. In the Gospel of Luke, the word friend has a positive connotation, but in the Gospel of Matthew the word friend has a negative connotation and really means something more like buster.[4] Thus, the King is saying, in essence, "Hey, buster, where's your tux?" The guest is speechless, and the king orders him to be thrown into the outer darkness, where there will be weeping and gnashing of teeth, which is an ancient Jewish way of saying that his life will unfold in endless tragedy.

If we were to survey the full scope of the Bible, we would notice an interesting preoccupation with what we wear. In the words of one preacher, the Bible begins with God dressing Adam and Eve in the Garden after their disobedience, and it ends with the saints being given white robes to wear in the

---

[3] Thomas G. Long, *Matthew* in the Westminster Bible Companion Series (Louisville: Westminster/John Knox Press, 1997), 246-247.

[4] Long, 247.

New Jerusalem. In between there is Paul's reminder to the Galatians that "as many of you as were baptized into Christ have clothed yourselves with Christ." Likewise, the Christians at Colossae, in a passage that is sometimes quoted at weddings, are told to clothe themselves with "compassion, kindness, humility, meekness, and patience."[5]

And in Matthew's version of Jesus' parable, the wedding robe itself represents the Christian life. In the words of preacher and writer Tom Long, the parable reminds us with urgency that being a part of the Christian community should make a discernible difference in who we are and how we live ...

> There should be a sense of awe and responsiveness about ... belonging to the community of Christ.... Sure, the spotlighted guest in the parable was pressed in off the street unexpectedly and was probably wearing cutoffs and [sneakers], but, when he got inside, only a fool would fail to see the difference between what he wore and where he was. He was in the banquet hall of the king; he was at the wedding feast of the royal son ... He is the recipient of *massive grace*. Where is his awe? Where is his wonder? Where is his regard for generosity? [The other guests have quietly traded] their street clothes for the garments of worship and celebration, but there he is bellying up to the punch bowl, stuffing his mouth with fig preserves, and

---

[5] From a sermon by Bob Dunham, preached at the University Presbyterian Church, Chapel Hill, North Carolina, October 9, 2011.

wiping his hands on his T-shirt. When the host demands to know where his wedding garment is, the man is speechless, and well he should be. In his self-absorption, he [hadn't fully realized] until that very moment that he was at a wedding banquet at all! Just so, to come into the church in response to the gracious and unmerited invitation of Christ and then not conform one's life to that mercy is to demonstrate a spiritual narcissism so profound that one cannot tell the difference between the wedding feast of the Lamb of God and happy hour in a bust station bar.[6]

Many commentators have suggested that the guests at an ancient Mediterranean wedding would have been provided with robes to wear, which perhaps explains the rage of the king upon discovering that this man had casually tossed his wedding robe onto a bar stool while taking advantage of the free booze.

For me, I'll admit that it makes the ending of the parable easier to swallow if the wayward guest had been given a robe to wear and then simply refused to wear it. But part of me wonders that even if he hadn't been provided with a robe, wouldn't his awe and gratitude in being invited to the royal wedding have been enough to motivate him to procure a robe? Wouldn't his awe and gratitude have been enough to spur him to new levels of ingenuity and creativity?

For most of my ministry I have preached a gospel of gracious

---

[6] Long, 247-248.

inclusion. All people are invited to the feast. God loves and cares for each one of us. Go out into the streets and invite still more people to come, because there is plenty of room in the banquet hall. And for anyone in the sound of my voice who needs to hear that message of gracious inclusion, I pray that is the message that you will hear.

But for those of us who have heard that message, for those of us who have responded to the invitation and find ourselves assembled in the great wedding hall, there is another message—namely, that if we truly comprehend what a marvelous thing it is to be included in the family of God then it will make a real difference in how we live our lives. The Gospel message is "Come as you are" not "come as you were." Grace is free, but it isn't cheap. It involves change, repentance.[7]

We have all been invited to the $500,000 per plate dinner that we could have never afforded on our own. The creative challenge before us is to figure out how to dress. Even if the tuxes and gowns are not passed out as we walk through the door, surely we have enough energy, intelligence, imagination, and love at our disposal to figure out how we can all help each other dress to the nines anyway.

Surely we have enough energy, intelligence, imagination, and love to help each other grow in our generosity, to help each other grow in our spiritual disciplines of prayer and Bible

---

[7] From a sermon preached by Lutheran pastor Elton Richards, entitled, "Sorry, I'm Busy," preached on the Day 1 Radio network, October 13, 1996.

reading, to help each other lead lives characterized by justice and integrity.

Surely the Holy Spirit is at work in each one of us, transforming us, molding us, until we look more and more like a wedding guest at the marriage feast of the Lamb of God.

In Keene, New Hampshire there is a facility named Cedarcrest that provides round-the-clock treatment for children with severe mental and developmental disabilities. Most families are too overwhelmed to provide that level of twenty-four-hour care at home. One Saturday I was making a pastoral visit to Cedarcrest with a family from our congregation in Vermont, and I noticed that all along the walls of the front hallway were pictures of the Cedarcrest children in evening gowns and tuxedos. One twelve-year-old boy had a jacket and tails draped over the back of his specialized wheelchair. Even the infant girls and boys were wearing gowns and tuxedos. I asked one of the staff members about the photographs, and she replied that they were the photos from the Cedarcrest Prom. I remarked how the staff must have spent hours custom fitting the formal wear and painstakingly dressing each child, not to mention all the other preparations for the prom. "Oh yes," she said, "but it was worth all the time and effort."

If you are ever invited to the Cedarcrest Prom, you wouldn't dare show up in a t-shirt and jeans.

The Gospel According to Birth Order

East Craftsbury Presbyterian Church
Craftsbury, Vermont
March 18, 2007

Now all the tax collectors and sinners were coming near to listen to him. And the Pharisees and the scribes were grumbling and saying, "This fellow welcomes sinners and eats with them." So he told them this parable: "Which one of you, having a hundred sheep and losing one of them, does not leave the ninety-nine in the wilderness and go after the one that is lost until he finds it? When he has found it, he lays it on his shoulders and rejoices. And when he comes home, he calls together his friends and neighbors, saying to them, 'Rejoice with me, for I have found my sheep that was lost.' Just so, I tell you, there will be more joy in heaven over one sinner who repents than over ninety-nine righteous persons who need no repentance. "Or what woman having ten silver coins, if she loses one of them, does not light a lamp, sweep the house, and search carefully until she finds it? When she has found it, she calls together her friends and neighbors, saying, 'Rejoice with me, for I have found the coin that I had lost.' Just so, I tell you, there is joy in the presence of the angels of God over one sinner who repents."

Then Jesus said, "There was a man who had two sons. The younger of them said to his father, 'Father, give me the share of the property that will belong to me.' So he divided his property between them. A few days later the younger son gathered all he had and traveled to a distant country, and there he squandered his property in dissolute living. When he had spent everything, a severe famine took place throughout that country, and he began to be in need. So he went and hired himself out to one of the citizens of that country, who sent him to his fields to feed the pigs. He would gladly have filled himself with the pods that the pigs were eating; and no one gave him anything. But when he came to himself he said, 'How many of my father's hired hands have bread enough and to spare, but here I am dying of hunger! I will get up and go to my father, and I will say to him, "Father, I have sinned against heaven and before you; I am no longer worthy to be called your son; treat me like one of your hired hands."' So he set off and went to his father. But while he was still far off, his father saw him and was filled with compassion; he ran and put his arms around him and kissed him. Then the son said to him, 'Father, I have sinned against heaven and before you; I am no longer worthy to be called your son.' But the father said to his slaves, 'Quickly, bring out a robe—the best one—and put it on him; put a ring on his finger and sandals on his feet. And get the fatted calf and kill it, and let us eat and celebrate; for this son of mine was dead and is alive again; he was lost and is found!' And they began to celebrate. "Now his elder son was in the field; and when he came and approached the house, he heard music and dancing. He called one of the slaves and asked what was going on. He replied, 'Your brother has come, and your father has killed the fatted calf, because he has got him back safe and sound.' Then he became angry and refused to go in. His father came out and *began to plead with him. But he answered his father, 'Listen! For all these years I have been working like a slave for you, and I have never disobeyed your command; yet you have never given me even a young goat so that I might celebrate with my friends. But when this son of yours came back, who has devoured your property with prostitutes, you killed the fatted calf for him!' Then the father said to him, 'Son, you are always with me, and all that is mine is yours. But we had to celebrate and rejoice, because this brother of yours was dead and has come to life; he was lost and has been found.'"*

—Luke 15:1-32

Today's story is one of the most beloved passages in all of scripture and also one of the most intensely disliked. It all depends on where you stand in the story. As Barbara Brown Taylor and others have pointed out, if you identify with the younger son, if you feel as if you were once lost but have now been found, if you have been haunted by mistakes for which you thought you could never be forgiven only to find yourself surprised by grace, then this is a story that you love with all your heart.

But if you identify with the older son, if you know what it means to work hard and be faithful to those who depend on you no matter what, if you know the pain of resentment that comes from watching other family members destroy everything you hold dear, then this is a story which at best leaves you deeply bewildered and at worst causes you to become enraged.

I've never been sure where I stand in this story, mostly because I'm an only child. I've often wondered what it might have been like to have had siblings. Would we have been close growing up? Or, if not, would we at least have grown closer to each other as adults, or would we still have found ourselves separated by a great gulf of physical and emotional distance? Who can say?

I've often sought out well-written narratives about brothers and sisters, trying to imagine where I might fit in such stories. One of my favorite and most deeply loved stories about two brothers is Norman Maclean's novella *A River Runs Through It*. Norman is the older brother, the one who goes to school in the East and then eventually becomes an English professor at the University of Chicago. Paul is the younger brother, the one who aspires to become a professional fly fisherman and who does a little reporting and newspaper work on the side. Unfortunately, Paul also has a tendency to drink heavily and engage in compulsive gambling. But unlike the younger son in the story which Jesus told, Paul refuses any help from his family, and he never once asks for money, not even when his gambling debts completely overwhelm him.

For the last two years I have taught *A River Runs Through It* in my "Spirituality of Place" course at Sterling College. Not too long ago I came across an essay written by English professor Grant T. Smith in which he describes the wide and various reactions that his students have had to reading that book through the years. One senior student named Beth wrote:

I can process intellectually how Paul may be considered a classical mythic western hero. He is a loner. He doesn't seek wealth or fame. He is self-sufficient. I can understand [why Maclean ascribes almost godlike qualities to Paul because of his great artistry as a fly fisherman.] I can appreciate all of this in my mind, but in my heart, I can only recognize my own brother, a narcissistic man who lived apart from his family from the time he turned eighteen.

Beth continues:

> Paul is the prodigal son, the favored son who is always welcomed back to the home despite whatever emotional damage he may have caused his family, especially his parents. Whenever there is a family reunion, it is Paul who is the central attraction. When Norman and Paul return to Missoula together, Norman says, 'Mother was especially nice to me, since she hadn't paid much attention to me so far,' but soon she was back with fresh rolls, and she buttered Paul's. She offers Paul chokecherry jelly, forgetting that it was Norman who liked that particular type of preserve.

Then Beth considers her own family, and she writes:

> The most vivid image I have of my mother is of her standing vigil at the kitchen window that faces the highway that runs past our house. She stands there waiting for my brother to come home. She cooks his favorite

meal; she washes the dishes; she waters the plants; she fusses over the curtains; she paces the floor. And always she looks out the window waiting for her son to come home, waiting until the darkness outside drives her finally to bed. On those rare occasions when my brother does pull into the driveway, on those rare occasions when he comes into the house sober and not stoned on alcohol, drugs, or both, my mother does precisely what Mrs. Maclean does. She warms up the meal she had prepared and then she laughs at his stories, because no one can tell stories and make people laugh like my brother can.

But as I said, those are the rare occasions. More often my brother doesn't show up at all, even though he had promised to be home. More often we get a call from the police or a friend instead of a call from my brother telling us that my brother once again has been in a fight, has shoplifted an item for beer money, has wrecked his car, has passed out in the park.

To me a hero is someone who goes through a journey. He gets the call, he goes on the journey, he has setbacks, but then he rises and returns and is celebrated. I don't find any of these qualities in Paul. I don't see any of these qualities in my brother.

Beth concludes her essay by asking:

Am I my brother's keeper? Can I say what the father in the book, the Reverend Maclean, says at the end of the story, 'you can love completely, even without complete understanding?'

No, I cannot . . . I have seen the hurt my own brother continues to inflict upon all of us in the family. He has left us nothing to celebrate. He has left only marks of hurt. We don't know him anymore. I can only echo the Reverend's final sentiments, 'It is those we live with and love and should know who elude us.'

After quoting Beth extensively, Professor Grant poses this question: "Is Beth's personal essay an example of a spiritual understanding of Maclean's novella, or does she miss completely the pathos of *A River Runs Through It?*" "I don't know," her professor says, "but perhaps Beth, by telling her story, is on a profound journey of healing."

And here ends my own very long quotation of Professor Grant's remarks. It occurs to me that through the years I have read and heard many sermons on the Prodigal Son, sermons which often describe the Prodigal's long journey from the far country back to his home. But Beth's essay helps remind me that the older son faces a very similar long journey home, even though he has never left the farm. If one son faces a long road in overcoming addictions, then the other son also faces a long road in overcoming ancient resentments and deep hurts. I don't know any shortcuts for either of these long roads. They are among the toughest and longest roads that any of us will ever have to travel.

No, I don't know any shortcuts. But maybe the secret to recovering a deep sense of joy can be heard in the Father's words in the parable when he says, "This brother of yours was dead and has come to life; he was lost and has been found."

A River Runs Through It is a hauntingly beautiful elegy for the brother who never came home. But the story of the Prodigal Son is a joy-filled story in which the lost brother does make his way home, and the deep hope at the end of the story is that the older brother, too, will make his way to the celebration.

I don't know where you stand in this story. I don't know whether you have already made your way to the celebration and the dancing, or whether you continue to stand outside, because there is still something about this story that rankles.

I can only say that in my own life I have found myself standing in both places. I have been the dutiful, older son who outwardly made his parents proud, and I have been the younger, prodigal son who avoided responsibility and ran away. I have heard people say that only children sometimes take on the characteristics of both older and younger siblings, and in my own life I have found this to be at least theologically true. I am the younger son, the refugee from the far country, the one who is surprised and overwhelmed with grace; and I am the older son, the one who stands outside and simply cannot forgive, especially when it comes to forgiving himself. And just as the father in the parable ran out to seek both sons, I found that whichever son I was, I was always welcomed back into my parent's house with open arms and with great joy.

I really am struck more and more by how the father runs out to find both sons. What we have in Luke chapter 15 is a parable of the Lost and Found. Luke introduced it by saying that Jesus told them a parable, not by saying Jesus told them three parables. Thus, the story of the lost sheep, the lost coin, the lost younger son, and, yes, the lost older son, all make up one contiguous parable of the lost and found. And whenever our God finds anyone who was lost, all of us are invited to the party.

Because, you see, somewhere in the center of our lives is the God who completely loves and completely understands us all, and who welcomes us, with open arms, into the house of joy.

Your Fair Share of the Rain

Westminster Presbyterian Church
Westminster, Colorado
September 18, 2011

"For the kingdom of heaven is like a landowner who went out early in the morning to hire laborers for his vineyard. After agreeing with the laborers for the usual daily wage, he sent them into his vineyard. When he went out about nine o'clock, he saw others standing idle in the marketplace; and he said to them, 'You also go into the vineyard, and I will pay you whatever is right.' So they went. When he went out again about noon and about three o'clock, he did the same. And about five o'clock he went out and found others standing around; and he said to them, 'Why are you standing here idle all day?' They said to him, 'Because no one has hired us.' He said to them, 'You also go into the vineyard.' When evening came, the owner of the vineyard said to his manager, 'Call the laborers and give them their pay, beginning with the last and then going to the first.' When those hired about five o'clock came, each of them received the usual daily wage. Now when the first came, they thought they would receive more; but each of them also received the usual daily wage. And when they received it, they grumbled against the landowner, saying, 'These last worked only one hour, and you have made them equal to us who have borne the burden of the day and the scorching heat.' But he replied to one of them, 'Friend, I am doing you no wrong; did you not agree with me for the usual daily wage? Take what belongs to you

and go; I choose to give to this last the same as I give to you. Am I not allowed to do what I choose with what belongs to me? Or are you envious because I am generous?' So the last will be first, and the first will be last."

—Matthew 20:1-16

I remember a scene in the movie "Matewan" in which this scripture passage was read. The narrator of the movie was a fifteen-year-old named Danny Radnor. He was a coal miner and a part-time Baptist preacher. He preached for both of the Baptist churches in this small town, the Hard-Shell and the Soft-Shell. The movie was set in 1920. It was a time when people were trying to organize West Virginia coal miners into a union. Danny's father had been killed in the mines. And so Danny was hoping that something could be done that would improve the conditions for workers in the mines. One night, Danny was preaching for the Hard-Shell Baptist Church, and after reading the same verses in Matthew's Gospel that we just read, he looks out into the congregation and says, "Now, it's clear from this parable that Jesus ain't heard nothing about the union! Because if he had, he would have changed his tune! Jesus would have said, 'the same dollar for the same work.'" And before Danny can say much more, the Hard-Shell pastor is chasing Danny out of the pulpit.

When we hear this parable, we're tempted to think there are all kinds of things that Jesus ain't heard nothing about. Jesus hasn't heard about what it's like to take classes in school where the expectation is that you attend classes every day, you do the work, you write whatever papers, you take a final, and then you get credit for the course. You do not simply show up on the last day of class and say, "Okay, I'd like my credit." That's not how it works.

Jesus also apparently never stood in line for the "Tower of Doom" ride at Elitches. All this business about the "last will be first and the first will be last" doesn't fly at amusement parks like Elitches or Disney World. Everywhere you go, you see signs that say, "Line cutting is cause for ejection from the park." There's something about this parable that just doesn't seem quite right. It just doesn't seem quite fair.

And as much as I've struggled with the adult sermon on this parable all week, I struggled even more over the children's sermon on this parable, which is why I finally opted to do the story about the manna with the children, instead. I was afraid of telling the Parable of the Laborers in the Vineyard to the children, especially because children have such an innate sense of fairness and justice. I had no idea how I would explain it to them. And, in some ways, I'm not sure how to explain it now.

And, in truth, we hear all the time that life isn't fair. It's one of those basic lessons that's supposed to instill character in us. It's just the way it is. Life isn't fair. Sometimes people get recognized for work they did not do, while others fail to get recognized for the work that they did. It's part of life. Life just isn't fair sometimes.

But as one preacher writes, "It is precisely because we know that life isn't fair that we expect that God should be."[8] Shouldn't God be the one who is fair? Shouldn't God be the one who is walking up and down the line, making sure that no one is taking cuts? Shouldn't God be the one that makes sure that everyone is being rewarded exactly for what they actually did and not for what people think they did or didn't do? Shouldn't God be the one who keeps score? And more than that, shouldn't God be the one who affords a basic measure of dignity and fairness?

Perhaps the cruelest part of the parable is when those who were hired first were made to wait at the end of the line to get their pay. They had bargained for the "usual daily wage"—a "denarius" in the Greek—just enough money to provide for their needs for that one day. They watch the others get paid, and they see that those who were hired last, who only worked an hour, also get the full, usual daily wage. A denarius. And then they brighten up, because all of a sudden, no longer is it a denarius for a day's work; it's now one denarius per hour! Twelve denarii![9]

And automatically they start calculating everything that twelve denarii will buy. Some of them are planning vacations. Others,

---

[8] From a famous sermon on this text by Barbara Brown Taylor, "Beginning at the End," in *The Seeds of Heaven: Sermons from the Episcopal Series of the Protestant Radio Hour* (Cincinnati: Forward Movement Publications, 1990), 77-78.

[9] Ibid. In her sermon Barbara Brown Taylor imagines a similar scene.

who are more prudent, are planning on how they can pay off their credit card bills and medical bills. Maybe they'll even have a little left over to put into the bank. And don't you know that even before they get to the end of the line, those twelve denarii have already been spent, which seems to make it all the more cruel when they only get a denarius apiece. All their hopeful expectations come crashing down, and you can hear the "thud" as they hit the ground. And it doesn't seem right. It seems, somehow, that their work is valued less than those who worked only an hour.

At the very beginning of the day, those who were first hired agreed to work for a denarius, or the usual daily wage. Everyone else agreed to work for what was right. And so at the very end of the exchange, the landowner reminds them that they bargained for a denarius, for the usual daily wage. And he says, "Friend, I am doing you no wrong. Did you not agree with me for the usual daily wage?"

You need to know something about the Gospel of Matthew. According to preacher and seminary professor Tom Long, when the Gospel of Matthew uses the word "friend," it is not a friendly term of address. It means something more like "buster," as in, "Listen to me, buster! Did you not get what you bargained for?"[10]

---

[10] For a discussion of the negative connotation of the word "friend" in Matthew's Gospel, see Thomas G. Long, *Matthew* (Louisville: Westminster/John Knox Press, 1997), 247.

Again, it seems cruel because we know that these first hired have worked all twelve hours in the scorching heat. But they bargained for the denarius, while the others agreed to work for what the landowner said was right.

That little denarius has so much power. It has the power to provide for daily needs, but it also has the power to measure our worth against other human beings, as if those who possess more denarii were somehow worth more as humans than those who possess less. And haven't we all seen good families torn apart by the influence of money?

One of the saddest stories I've heard was told by a preacher who was vacationing in Mexico with his family. He and his family were having dinner in an open-air patio. Next to them was a couple from the States. Nearby were children who were selling chewing gum and begging in the market place. The man, sitting next to them, had pesos, and he called the children and said, "If you run around the plaza as fast as you can and as long as you can, I'll give you a peso each." And so the little boys started running. They ran around the plaza. The man just laughed, and kept yelling, "Corre, corre", which is Spanish for run!"[11]

---

[11] Story told by Presbyterian minister (and now seminary president) Ted Wardlaw, as quoted in Charles Campbell, *The Word Before the Powers: An Ethic of Preaching* (Louisville: Westminster/John Knox Press, 2002), 115.

Isn't it funny how that same denarius, that same peso, that same dollar, that has the power to convey a sense of dignity and worth, also has the power to take it away?

I think it makes all the difference in the world whether you bargained for the denarius, or whether you went into the vineyard on the word of him who said, "I will pay you what is right." Is our trust in the denarius or in a good and generous God who is always going out to the marketplace, always seeking to see if there is anyone who needs work?"

You see, those who were last hired also bore the brunt of the day in the scorching sun. Only they did it in the marketplace, not knowing if they would ever get hired or not, not knowing if they would be able to provide for their family that day or not. Whereas those who worked twelve hours in the field, as hard as they worked, at least they knew they would be getting paid at the end of the day.[12]

Last night, we had a celebration for the Presbytery of Denver. We were celebrating Tom Sheffield's tenth anniversary as the Presbytery Pastor. There was a lot of food. Emma and I arrived a little bit late, and we were at the very end of the line. And then we saw Bruce Spear, the former interim pastor of this congregation, who joined us at the end of the line. It was great

---

[12] I am unable to recall the original source for this insight. I believe it may have come from a sermon by the late George Buttrick (1892-1980).

to see Bruce. And Bruce said, "Ah, the last will be first, and the first will be last."

And then I said, "Are you preaching on that parable tomorrow, too? Because I could use some tips."

And Bruce replied, "Oh, is that parable tomorrow? I'm not following the lectionary these days."

And I said, "I see."

And we had some more conversations with other people in line. And then, the next thing I knew, I looked around and Bruce wasn't there anymore. I looked around some more, and I finally spotted Bruce all the way at the head of the line. And I thought, "How did that happen? He's not even preaching on this parable tomorrow!" And so, Bruce had been last, and now he was first. And Emma and I started out last, and we were still last! But do you know how much those at the end of the line got to eat compared to those at the first of the line? Just as much. There was plenty of food for everyone.

You see, if all you see is a denarius. If all you know is the market value of that denarius, then all you know is the economic worth. But if you trust the one who sends you into the vineyard, then you know that the usual daily wage—the denarius—means something entirely different. It means your fair share of all God's good provisions![13]

---

[13] Long, 226.

Tom Long puts it this way: "There you are, standing in a torrential rain, getting utterly drenched in God's mercy and grace. Do you then whine that you're not getting your fair share of the rain?"[14]

Every month, on the third Thursday, we host a community dinner. And as we have come to know the guests that come each month, we know that many of them struggle with full employment. Many of them have been looking for jobs for months on end, often without any helpful leads. They never know if they will have enough to provide for themselves and their families. Every day they live in a world where the power of the denarius, the power of the dollar, weighs heavily upon them. It impinges upon their sense of worth.

But when we share a meal together as a church, when we welcome them as guests, we are getting a glimpse of the Kingdom of Heaven, where there is no distinction between first and last. Nor is there any distinction between those who are serving and those who are being served. Everyone sits at table alike and experiences a foretaste of that great banquet when "they will come from east and west, and from north and south, and sit at table in the Kingdom of Heaven." (Luke 13:29).

A friend of mine went to a very competitive medical school. The air was thick with the spirit of competition. People were always trying to size each other up. "Where do *you* rank?" They

---

[14] Ibid.

were obsessed with keeping tabs on who was up and who was down. One day, one of their professors addressed the whole class, and he said, "Do you know what they call the person who graduates dead last in this program? . . . Doctor!"

What do you suppose they call the person who is dead last in the Kingdom of Heaven?

A beloved child of God.

Don't Ask Me What It Means. I Don't Know.

East Craftsbury Presbyterian Church
Craftsbury, Vermont
September 19, 2004

Then Jesus said to the disciples, "There was a rich man who had a manager, and charges were brought to him that this man was squandering his property. So he summoned him and said to him, 'What is this that I hear about you? Give me an accounting of your management, because you cannot be my manager any longer.' Then the manager said to himself, 'What will I do, now that my master is taking the position away from me? I am not strong enough to dig, and I am ashamed to beg. I have decided what to do so that, when I am dismissed as manager, people may welcome me into their homes.' So, summoning his master's debtors one by one, he asked the first, 'How much do you owe my master?' He answered, 'A hundred jugs of olive oil.' He said to him, 'Take your bill, sit down quickly, and make it fifty.' Then he asked another, 'And how much do you owe?' He replied, 'A hundred containers of wheat.' He said to him, 'Take your bill and make it eighty.' And his master commended the dishonest manager because he had acted shrewdly; for the children of this age are more shrewd in dealing with their own generation than are the children of light. And I tell you, make friends for yourselves by means of dishonest wealth so that when it is gone, they may welcome you into the eternal homes. "Whoever is faithful in a very little is faithful also in much; and whoever is dishonest in a very little is dishonest also in much. If then you have not been faithful with the dishonest wealth, who will entrust to you the true riches? And if you have not been faithful with what belongs to another, who will give you what is your own? No slave can serve two masters; for a slave will either hate the one and love the other, or be devoted to the one and despise the other. You cannot serve God and wealth."

—Luke 16:1-13

There's a scene in "Cinema Paradiso," one of my favorite movies, where the elderly film projectionist Alfredo is telling a story to his young friend Toto, who has become very much like a son to him, especially since Toto's own father had been killed in World War II. Alfredo tells the story with such great feeling that Toto is completely entranced, and then the story has a surprising and confusing twist, and Alfredo stops talking. Toto waits for a while and then asks, "So, how does it end?" And Alfredo replies, "That was the end. And don't ask me what it means. I don't know. When you figure out, you tell me."

That's how I feel about preaching on this morning's parable. It's very tempting for me to read the lesson, close the Bible, and then say, "I don't know what it means. When you figure out, you tell me." End of sermon. Sit down.

The parable of the dishonest manager or the unjust steward has baffled interpreters since the beginning of time, or at least since Jesus first told the story.

Once upon a time, Jesus said, there was a rich man who had a steward, a kind of business manager, and charges were brought to the man that his manager was wasting his goods. It's not clear if the manager was stealing from his boss or if he was just a very bad manager. The manager was called in and told, "You're fired!"

But for some reason the manager is allowed a few days to audit the books before he turns them back in. Meanwhile, the manager went around to all the rich man's debtors and cooked the books. He discounted what everybody owed, that way they would be so grateful to him that perhaps later on they would help him out a little bit in his impending unemployment. In order for the scheme to work, the debtors must not yet know that the manager has been fired. Therefore, they must assume that the landowner himself has authorized all the mark downs. The master hopes that all of his master's debtors will remember that he was the bearer of the good news.

Another mystery is whether the manager was simply cutting out his own commission or whether he was making lavish deductions and thereby in a sense stealing even more from his master. And then the most surprising thing is that the landowner praises the manager. So, this, then is the confusing story of the employee who duped his employer only to receive lavish praise from the very employer he had just duped.

And don't ask me what it means. I don't know.

Many commentators have surmised that the Gospel writer

Luke had as much trouble understanding this parable as we do. In writing his Gospel, Luke assembles together different sayings by Jesus in the verses following this parable. In doing so, Luke seems to offer three different ways to explain the meaning of the parable. The first is do like the shady steward and make friends with unrighteous money—whatever that means! —so that when it fails you'll have friends in high places. The second is you must do well with a little or you won't be entrusted with more, which makes sense, but I'm not sure how it relates to the parable. And the third is you can't serve God and money, so make a choice. Again, that's an understandable point, but it's not clear how that relates to the parable, either.

Preachers and interpreters are all over the map in trying to explain this parable. Some interpreters suggest that perhaps Jesus is using humor or irony that we miss somehow because we don't pick up on all the cultural cues. Frederick Buechner suggests that Jesus' use of humor is intentional, and he compares Jesus' parable-telling to a kind of joke telling. When Buechner suggests that Jesus is joking, he's not saying that we shouldn't take Jesus seriously; rather, he's saying that Jesus is telling us that we shouldn't take ourselves too seriously.[15] Once the rug is pulled out from under our feet, we realize that we were never able to stand on our own two feet in the first place, and that all of us are utterly dependent on the surprising grace of God.

---

[15] Frederick Buechner, *Telling the Truth: The Gospel as Tragedy, Comedy, and Fairy Tale* (HarperSanFrancisco, 1977), 66-70.

I once quoted Buechner on joke telling in a sermon I preached as a seminary intern in Vallejo, California, and after the worship service a retired preacher in the congregation offered to take me out to lunch. During the lunch, he turned to me and said, "Young man, Jesus doesn't joke!" In truth, I still think that Buechner is right about Jesus using humor to disarm us and encourage us not to take ourselves too seriously, but I've learned I could be more cautious about stating that Jesus was a joke teller. And I'm not sure that simply stating that Jesus was a joke teller helps us all that much with today's parable, because we're obviously not in on the joke.

Another interpretation I've heard is that this story encourages us to get our hands dirty. In other words, we shouldn't be so "spiritual" that we are afraid to become involved in the nitty gritty of the world. I'm reminded of a minister friend of mine who knows a lawyer in Texas who works for one of the big downtown firms. The lawyer does a lot of pro bono work in behalf of tenants. If he gets wind of landlords using unfair practices, he writes them a very intimidating letter using the stationery of the big, downtown law firm. That's often enough to get the landlords to change their tune. As the lawyer tells about this, he puts his boots up on the desk, and exclaims with a thick Texas drawl, "I just love working for justice."

I've even heard one interpretation of this parable that suggests that the very ambiguity of the parable is the point. Life isn't always cut and dried. It's often very ambiguous.[16] End of sermon. Sit down.

One intriguing interpretation comes from a Presbyterian pastor and former missionary named Kenneth Bailey, who taught for many years in Beirut, Lebanon. While he was there, Bailey made a number of observations about Middle Eastern peasant culture that he then used in his study of Jesus' parables.[17] Like I said, I find Bailey's interpretation intriguing, but I'm not persuaded it's right. Historians warn us not to make assumptions about the past based on our experiences of the present. Bailey's observations about present-day Middle Eastern culture may or may not be applicable to the Middle Eastern peasant culture of Jesus' day. Where Bailey's interpretations are helpful is in helping us understand how contemporary Middle Easterners might hear Jesus' parables.

According to Bailey, the manager experiences grace from his employer from the very beginning. The manager could have been thrown in jail for his mismanagement, so, when he is merely fired, he experienced grace. Then the manager acted quickly to reduce all the debts, and now all the debtors believe that the landowner, acting through the manager, is the most

---

[16] I'm oversimplifying an approach taken by David Buttrick in a sermon entitled "On the Virtue of Being a Crook / Ambiguity" in *The Pulpit Digest*, January — March 2000.

[17] Kenneth E. Bailey, *Poet & Peasant and Through Peasant Eyes: A Literary-Cultural Approach to the Parables in Luke, Combined Edition* (Grand Rapids: Wm. B. Eerdmans, 1976, 1980), 86-109.

generous man ever to rent land in the country. Anywhere someone raises a glass, they are toasting the rich man's generosity. The rich man is trapped. There is no way to say, "Very sorry, it was all a mistake." In Middle Eastern culture, you simply cannot do that. He would be hated forever if he tried to repeal the reductions. The rich man has to honor all the reductions, and so he praises the manager for acting shrewdly.

According to Bailey, the manager, having experienced grace at the very beginning of the story, decides to gamble that he will receive even more grace from the master. He gambles everything on his belief that his master will not throw him in jail, even after he steals even more from his master by reducing everyone's debts.

Bailey's interpretation, right or wrong, reminds me of a scene from *Les Misérables*. Jean Valjean spends nineteen years in prison for stealing a loaf of bread and for repeatedly trying to escape from prison. When he is finally paroled, he must wear special identification at all times, which means that he experiences ridicule wherever he goes and it's impossible for him to find a job. Jean Valjean is taken in by a bishop and given a meal and lodging for the night. But in the middle of the night, Jean Valjean steals two silver candlesticks and sneaks out. The townspeople capture him and threaten to turn him in to the bishop. Valjean lies and says that the silver candlesticks were a gift. Like the dishonest manager in the parable, perhaps, Valjean gambles on the kindness he has already received from the bishop. And then comes the surprise. The bishop arrives and says, "That's right, the candlesticks were a gift, but you forgot that I also gave you all this other silverware as well. Why would you leave the best pieces behind?" And then, after the townspeople have left, the bishop turns to Valjean and says, "I have bought your life for God. Use this silver to become an honest man." I don't know if Bailey's interpretation is right or not, but I love stories that end on a surprising note of grace.

Lastly, I'd like to share what is probably the least controversial interpretation of this parable. It's also perhaps one of the simplest as well as most challenging interpretations. This interpretation has to do with time. What the manager realizes is that the does not have forever, that the accounts are being called in, and he must show what he's done. While he's not a paragon of virtue, he does know what time it is. He doesn't sit on his hands and starve. He comes up with a plan. And so he goes to each of his master's debtors, and says, "Sit down quickly. Hurry. Quickly, write this down." He knows that he doesn't have much time, and that's perhaps the most poignant lesson he should teach us.[18]

Michael Christofer's play *The Shadow Box* portrays patients and family members at a hospice treatment center. Near the end of the drama the characters break the fourth wall to speak directly

---

[18] This point was made in a famous sermon by Edmund Steimle entitled, "Sit Down Quickly," and more recently in a sermon by Jon Walton entitled, "Blessed are the Clever" in *Imperfect Peace: Teaching Sermons on Troubling Texts* (Nashville: Abingdon Press, 1999), 109-112.

to the audience. One by one they say that someone should have told them that life doesn't last forever. They wonder what a difference it might have made earlier on, if someone had appeared on the scene to tell them that life doesn't last.[19]

I'm not sure why Jesus told the parable of the Dishonest Manager. It is still the most confusing story Jesus ever told. But in the words of preacher Jon Walton:

> No one has ever had a better sense of time than Jesus did, no better awareness that one life can do so much for good or ill, and that we don't have forever to do it. For Jesus time was always too short, and when that time came for him to die, it was too soon.
>
> Is it any different for us? The accounts are always called in too soon.[20]

Dear friends, whatever we believe we are called to do, we should do it quickly.

---

[19] Michael Christofer, *The Shadow Box*, as summarized in a sermon by Patrick J. Willson, "Time for Champagne and Wisdom," in *Pulpit Digest*, January - March 2000.

[20] Walton, 112.

Risking a New Beginning

Jack Cabaness

Sermons on the Book of Job

Risking a New Beginning

Have You Considered My Servant Job?

Westminster Presbyterian Church
Westminster, Colorado
October 7, 2012

There was once a man in the land of Uz whose name was Job. That man was blameless and upright, one who feared God and turned away from evil.

One day the heavenly beings came to present themselves before the LORD, and Satan also came among them to present himself before the LORD. The LORD said to Satan, "Where have you come from?" Satan answered the LORD, "From going to and fro on the earth, and from walking up and down on it." The LORD said to Satan, "Have you considered my servant Job? There is no one like him on the earth, a blameless and upright man who fears God and turns away from evil. He still persists in his integrity, although you incited me against him, to destroy him for no reason." Then Satan answered the LORD, "Skin for skin! All that people have they will give to save their lives. But stretch out your hand now and touch his bone and his flesh, and he will curse you to your face." The LORD said to Satan, "Very well, he is in your power; only spare his life."

So Satan went out from the presence of the LORD, and inflicted loathsome sores on Job from the sole of his foot to the crown of his head. Job took a potsherd with which to scrape himself, and

> *sat among the ashes. Then his wife said to him, "Do you still persist in your integrity? Curse God, and die." But he said to her, "You speak as any foolish woman would speak. Shall we receive the good at the hand of God, and not receive the bad?" In all this Job did not sin with his lips.*
>
> —Job 1:1; 2:1-10

It's hard to say, "Thanks be to God," when you have a reading from the book of Job. As I said a moment ago, this is one of the more difficult books for Jews and Christians alike. It has puzzled interpreters for a long time.

And as I try to preach on the Book of Job, I'm reminded of something a Lutheran pastor and preaching professor named Edmund Steimle once said. Steimle actually used to summer in Vermont not far from where Emma and I used to live, although he was in Vermont many years before we were. Steimle was a teacher of preachers, and he would often tell his students how to think of a good sermon. Steimle said, "A good sermon is *not* a pretty package neatly wrapped up and tied with a bow. A good sermon is more like the rings on the surface of a lake where the preacher has gone down into deep water." And I hope that Steimle was right because, I should tell you, that as I prepare to preach on the book of Job, I feel like I'm way in over my head.[21]

---

[21] I have heard this anecdote about Steimle on several occasions, but most recently I was reminded of it by preaching professor Thomas G. Long in

I think that we all are when we ponder these hard, difficult questions. If God is all-loving and all-powerful, why do the innocent suffer? We can reconcile any two of those statements pretty easily. Reconciling all three of those statements is difficult. Maybe the innocent suffer because God is all-loving but not all-powerful? Or maybe the innocents suffer because God is all-powerful but not all loving? But if we insist that God is both all-powerful and all-loving, it is hard for us to understand why the innocent suffer.

According to the text, Job is blameless before God, and yet, for some reason, he is allowed to suffer immensely. These are hard questions. And I don't pretend that we will answer them this morning. But I hope that we will find ways of faithfully living with these questions. We'll explore these questions more in depth on the remaining Sundays in October as we go through the book of Job. But in all honestly, we're in over our heads. We're in deep water as we try to sit with Job.

And there are mysteries here. Even the brief conversation between Job and his wife is ambiguous. In the translation that we read a moment ago, she tells Job, "Do you still insist on your integrity? Curse God and die!" However, if you go to the original Hebrew, that word "curse" is actually the word "bless." And some scholars feel that she probably really meant "curse." It's just that the ancient scribes did not even want to

---

his third lecture for the 2009 Currie Lectures given at Austin Presbyterian Theological Seminary.

write down the words "curse God" on a scroll. And so they wrote the word "bless" as a euphemism for the word "curse."[22]

Are you confused yet? Are we in deep water, or what? Old Testament scholar Sam Balentine suggests that perhaps the word "bless" is intended to mean bless, and that it's not simply a euphemism for the word "curse." It could be that Job's wife is not sarcastic at all. Instead, she goes up to Job and says, "You've suffered enough. You *are* a man of integrity. No one can blame you now. **Bless** God and die. It's okay to let go. You can let go now." It could be that that's what she was saying to Job. That's not the traditional interpretation. But it's possible.

Whether Job's wife sought to be sarcastic or soothing, she ends up agitating Job. Who among us here has not tried to soothe someone we love with comforting words only to receive a harsh rebuke? The very words that did seem to be comforting to someone else in another situation are suddenly not comforting now.

We're in deep water here. And we might as well admit that we're in deep water and that Job raises hard questions. And these are important questions, because we're talking about real people.

Not too long ago someone called me up on the church phone asking for assistance. And he compared his struggles to the

---

[22] These observations are from Old Testament scholar Samuel Balentine in his magisterial commentary on the Book of Job. See Samuel Balentine, *Job* (Macon, Georgia: Smyth & Helwys, 2006), 49.

struggles of Job. And as I listened, I was a little skeptical, thinking that perhaps he might be prone to a little bit of hyperbole. But then again, who am I to judge? I don't dare second-guess another person's story of suffering because I don't really know. But I can tell you about the time that I met the real Job in person. His name is Jose Antonio. And he lives in Nicaragua. Many of you have heard me mention him before because I am haunted by him. He shows up in my sermons at least once a year.

I was able to travel with my seminary classmates to Nicaragua in January of 1999, which was just about six weeks after Hurricane Mitch absolutely devastated the country. What happened was that Hurricane Mitch came over Nicaragua and just hovered there for five or six days, raining as in the days of Noah. And the floods were devastating. There was this one village north of Managua that was near an extinct volcano and that ancient crater filled completely with water and then the entire mountain collapsed. And the ensuing mudslide wiped out an entire village.

We were able to see this devastation first hand. We met Jose Antonio and he was telling us that he lost his whole family. Like Job, he had lost his entire family. He had been searching for weeks and hadn't found a trace of any of them. And then he said, "*No tengo ningún consuelo que Dios.*" (Translation: I have no consolation but God). And he said that in a tone of voice that was poignant and sad, but also hopeful, as if to say, "I have no consolation but God, but from the very depth of my being, I know that somehow that will be enough." I have no consolation but God.

A few days later we celebrated communion in Managua, the capital city, not far from where the ruins of the 1972 earthquake can still be seen, still not rebuilt after all those years, and not far from the shores of Lake Managua, which was quite polluted. And yet, in that communion service, we might as well have been on the shore of the Lake of Galilee with Jesus himself, as he fed all the disciples, as he fed Jose Antonio, as he fed all of us.

And for all the Jobs in the world who are scraping themselves with a piece of broken pottery, symbolizing all that's broken, all that was once whole and is now shattered. For all the Jobs in the world, scraping themselves with broken pottery, in an attempt to distract themselves from the pain. For all the Jobs in the world, there is an invitation from the Lord Jesus, who meets us here at this table in his own brokenness and invites us to partake in this meal that he has prepared.

Now this is not an attempt to wrap the sermon up in pretty packaging and tie it up with a bow. It is not a promise that we will come up with satisfying answers for all the difficult questions that Job raises. But what it means is that as we live faithfully with these questions, as we continue to be faithful in prayer, we can keep coming to this table again and again, in our brokenness. And one who was broken for our sakes will meet us here.

The Patience of Job

Westminster Presbyterian Church
Westminster, Colorado
October 14, 2012

Then Job answered: "Today also my complaint is bitter; his hand is heavy despite my groaning. Oh, that I knew where I might find him, that I might come even to his dwelling! I would lay my case before him, and fill my mouth with arguments. I would learn what he would answer me, and understand what he would say to me. Would he contend with me in the greatness of his power? No; but he would give heed to me. There an upright person could reason with him, and I should be acquitted forever by my judge.

"If I go forward, he is not there; or backward, I cannot perceive him; on the left he hides, and I cannot behold him; I turn to the right, but I cannot see him. God has made my heart faint; the Almighty has terrified me; If only I could vanish in darkness, and thick darkness would cover my face!

—Job 23:1-9, 16-17

At the very beginning of the Book of Job, Job is portrayed as the wealthiest and most righteous man in the land of Uz. No one knows where that was. It's like the beginning of Star Wars: "A long time ago, in a galaxy far, far away." It's meant to evoke the sense of an ancient story. It's meant to suggest that Job could be anyone across time and space. This is a story that we know, even if we can't find Uz on a map.[23]

As the story begins, Job is interrupted by a messenger who says, "The oxen were plowing and the donkeys were grazing and the Sabeans came and took them and killed the boys and only I escaped to tell you."

And then, before that messenger is finished speaking, another messenger comes and says, "Lightning fell from the sky and burned up the sheep and the boys and only I escaped to tell you."

And then before that messenger is finished speaking, still another comes and says, "The Chaldeans attacked the camels and took them and killed the boys and only I escaped to tell you."

And before that messenger is finished speaking, still another comes and says, "Your sons and daughters were feasting and a great wind came out of the desert and knocked down the walls of the house and it fell on them and they're dead and only I escaped to tell you."

Wave after wave of bad news. Stephen Mitchell, who has done his own translation of the Book of Job, says that this is tragi-

---

[23] See comments by J. Gerald Janzen, *Job*, Interpretation Commentaries (Atlanta: John Knox Press, 1985), 34.

comic puppet theater which is meant to *heighten* the sense of tragedy.[24] It's intended as a dramatic device. I can appreciate that insight from a literary point of view, but to me Job feels more like real life and less like dramatic hyperbole. Sadly, many of us do know what it's like when tragedy compounds upon tragedy.

For those of us here in Colorado, a messenger came early in the summer and said, "There's a wildfire raging out of control to the north in Hyde Park."

And before that messenger finished speaking, another messenger came and said, "There's another wildfire to the south in Waldo Canyon."

And before that messenger finished speaking, another messenger came and said, "There's been a tragic shooting at a theater in Aurora."

And before that messenger finished speaking, another messenger came and said, "There's a missing ten-year-old girl in Westminster."

And before that messenger had finished speaking, another came and said, "I'm sorry to tell you that she's dead."

---

[24] Stephen Mitchell, *The Book of Job* (San Francisco: North Point Press, 1987), xii.

Yes, we know what it's like to experience tragedy after tragedy. We're not even done grieving the first tragedy when more bad news arrives.

That's where we find Job, and then his friends appear. And before I criticize his friends—which I will do in the course of this sermon—I want to tell you first what the friends did right. When Job's friends first encounter him, they sit down with him. And they don't say a thing for seven days and seven nights. They don't even try to give him some cheap bumper sticker theology, *at least not at first!* They actually sit down with Job in silence. And there is much, much to be said about presence. If you're not sure what to say to a grieving friend, that's okay. Sit down with them. Spend time with them. Help them out in whatever way possible. You cannot overestimate the importance of a ministry of presence.

But after the seven days, the friends begin to speak, and that is when the problems start. Preaching professor Tom Long describes Job's friends in this way:

> The first is Eliphaz, who is the embodiment of a mushy brand of self-serving piety . . . Eliphaz takes one look at Job and says, "Sin has seduced your mind. You are lucky God has scolded you. If I were you, I would pray. [*Never mind that Job has been praying all his life, but Eliphaz looks at Job, and says, "Job, I think you should pray.*] Make peace with God and you will not be sorry.

The maddening thing about Eliphaz is that he has turned some of the faith's strongest affirmations into cross-stitched slogans suitable for hanging on the wall. To Eliphaz, the power of prayer is a bargaining chip, peace with God a negotiating device. He does not have faith; he has a religion machine.

[And then along comes Bildad]. Bildad is a religious authoritarian. He has a bumper sticker on his car that reads, "God said it. I believe it. And that's that." Bildad views human nature as a bowl of spoiled mayonnaise, describing humanity as "that worm, that vile, stinking maggot." And he's never been there himself, but Bildad can confidently tell us what goes on in college dormitories, denominational headquarters, the house next door, and every other cesspool of iniquity... And it's no surprise then that Bildad tells Job, "Well, Job, your children must have sinned. And so all of you are getting the punishment that you deserve."

[And then along comes Zophar]. Zophar is a Bildad who has gone to seminary. Zophar is there, smoking his pipe, at the very time that Job is scratching a boil with a shard of broken pottery. And Zophar says, "You know, Job, you just don't understand that you're a sinner. You just don't understand that you're a sinner." And then Zophar says, "A stupid man will be wise when a cow gives birth to a zebra." That's the comfort that Zophar tries to give Job.[25]

And in Stephen Mitchell's translation, Job turns to his friends, and speaks to them, dripping with sarcasm, as he says:

> "How kind you have all been to me! How considerate of my pain! What would I do without you and the good advice you have given me? Who has made you so tactful and inspired such compassionate words?"

And then Job says:

> "I swear by God, who has wronged me and filled my cup with despair, that while there is life in this body and as long as I can breathe, I will never let you convict me; I will never give up my claim. I will hold tight to my innocence; my mind will never submit."[26]

And so throughout the Book of Job, Job insists upon his integrity. He insists that he has done nothing wrong. He insists on getting a hearing with God and having a chance to complain to God that he has been treated unfairly. As Job says, "My complaint is bitter. My complaint is defiant." And as Eugene

---

[25] Thomas G. Long, *What Shall We Say?: Evil, Suffering, and the Crisis of Faith* (Grand Rapids: Wm. B. Eerdmans, 2011), 102-104.

[26] Mitchell, *The Book of Job*, 64. Here, Mitchell summarizes Job's speech in chapters 26 and 27.

Peterson renders it in *The Message*, "My complaint is legitimate."

If you've read ahead in the Book of Job, you know what happens. God finally speaks, and God turns to the three friends who are speaking so confidently about the will of God to give humans free will, even if that means they choose evil and cause suffering, and how all that means that Job must have done something wrong. These friends' theme song is the opposite of "The Sound of Music." Instead of singing, "I Must Have Done Something Good," they're serenading Job and singing, "Job, somewhere in your youth or childhood, you must have done something wrong!"

But God points to those three friends and says, "No! Job's not wrong! You're wrong! Job has spoken right." Isn't that remarkable? God vindicates the one who dared to speak out and criticizes the ones who mouthed the pious party line.

We'll have more to say about Job's dialogue with God next week, but suffice it to say for now that God vindicates Job, and God vindicates Job's right to ask the hard questions, even if those hard questions are asked with a raised fist.

The Book of James has this famous quotation: "You've heard of the patience of Job." (James 5:11). Isn't that an odd thing to say? Patience?!? Really? Did you not hear Job rage against his friends and against God? You're calling Job patient?

In James's defense, the Greek word that the King James Translators translated as "patience" is probably best translated as "endurance" or "persistence." Nonetheless, "the patience of Job" is part of our lexicon.

This is what I think about when I think about "the patience of Job." Job prays his honest and heart-felt prayer to God, saying, "God, why did you let this happen to me? None of it makes sense!"

But then Job doesn't walk away. Job comes back, and he prays again, "God, this isn't fair. I need you to make sense of this."

And then Job still doesn't walk away. He comes back, and he prays again. Job is like that pastor who one day interrupted the congregation's recitation of the Lord's Prayer by interjecting, "Lord, we pray that every single week, and yet the children still go hungry and war wages on." This was right after all the voices in unison had said, "Give us this day our daily bread."

And Job still persists. He prays again and again, "Lord, I did nothing wrong. I need you to make sense of my suffering. I need my redeemer to come, at long last."

And, now, do you begin to see why Job was patient?

Behemoth in a Hamster Wheel

Westminster Presbyterian Church
Westminster, Colorado
October 21, 2012

Then the LORD *answered Job out of the whirlwind:*
'Who is this that darkens counsel by words without knowledge?
Where were you when I laid the foundation of the earth?
  Tell me, if you have understanding.
Who determined its measurements—surely you know!

Has the rain a father,
  or who has begotten the drops of dew?
From whose womb did the ice come forth,
  and who has given birth to the hoar-frost of heaven?
The waters become hard like stone,
  and the face of the deep is frozen.

Can you bind the chains of the Pleiades,
  or loose the cords of Orion?'

—Job 38:1-2, 4-5, 28-30, 31

In 1915, the British explorer Ernest Shackleton was hoping that his expedition would be the first to traverse the continent of Antarctica from one shore to the next. The race to the South Pole itself had already been won, but Shackleton was hoping that his crew would be the first to go across the entire continent. But before they really got started, their ship got marooned in pack ice, and he realized that they would have to abandon ship.

So Shackleton ordered all of his men to take no more than two pounds of survival gear and a personal diary. Shackleton himself got rid of his gold sovereigns and his watch. He even left behind the ship's Bible, which had been given to him by the Queen Mother. But before he abandoned ship, he took out a single page from the Bible. Just one page. Any guesses as to what that one page might have been?

Well, since this is a sermon on the 38th chapter of the Book of Job, if you were to guess something from Job 38, you would be right!

> *Out of whose womb came the ice*
> *and the hoary frost of Heaven, who hast gendered it?*
> —Job 38:29, King James Version

A very appropriate verse in that Antarctic setting!

Who knows how strong a personal faith Ernest Shackleton himself had, but he was living in an era when many people knew their Bible very well. Can you imagine finding that particular page of scripture on a moment's notice? Shackleton took that one page containing the 38th chapter of the Book of Job, and it accompanied them all through the dangerous expedition in the lifeboats back to the southern coast of New Zealand.

But why that page? Why the 38th chapter of Job? A moment ago, I heard somebody shout out the 23rd Psalm. Wouldn't that have been a more appropriate choice to take with you on the long journey? Wouldn't you seek a shepherd's rod and staff to protect you from the rocks and ice on the dangerous sea voyage back to New Zealand?

Or maybe you would have picked the eighth chapter of Romans with its assurances that all things work together for good and that there is nothing in life or in death or in all creation that can separate us from the love of God in Christ Jesus our Lord. Wouldn't you have rather had Psalm 23 or Romans 8 for the journey?

Instead, Shackleton took a chapter out of the Bible that is short on direct assurances and long on rhetorical questions, including questions such as, "Have you entered the storehouses of the snow?" That's one of my favorite phrases from that chapter. Wouldn't all of the Colorado ski operators love to have access to the storehouses of snow? If they were having a bad winter with not enough snow, they could just ask God to open up the storehouses and send more. I like that. It's beautiful poetry. But is it sustaining? Is it the kind of answer I would need in my darkest hour?

Here's another passage from Job 38: "Can you bind the chains of Pleiades or loose the cords of Orion?" Those verses appeal to me because of my own interest in astronomy. Once again, it's beautiful, beautiful poetry. But is it enough to take with you on the journey through the darkest valley?

This month, I'm remembering a friend of mine from Vermont, named Delbert. He was in his early '90s. He lived in the assisted living facility that was across the road from the church I served in Vermont. Every Friday, I would go and lead a Bible study, and Delbert was always there. He was a wonderful storyteller. He had been a truck driver for Patton's armies during World War II. And to hear Delbert tell it, he drove all across Europe in a truck that had no shock absorbers and hardly any cushion in the driver's seat.

Thus, I had a mental picture of Delbert driving all across Europe in a truck that was constantly getting rattled. But I never knew how to take Delbert's stories because he also used to tell me that the Vermont winters of his youth were much, much worse than the winters of today, and that he could remember driving a truck across the frozen surface of Lake Caspian . . . *in June*. So, I never knew how much stock to put in the literal details of Delbert's stories.

Six years ago this month, the phone rang at three in the morning. It was my doctor. And since we lived in a small town, my doctor was my neighbors' doctor, too. He told me that Delbert was dying, and his family couldn't get there and could I please come across the street and sit with Delbert? And so I did. I sat with him while he was dying.

And shortly after he passed away, I looked more closely at newspaper clippings that Delbert had posted on his walls. I found one article with the headline, "Where Was God?" I started reading the article and saw that it was about WWII veterans who had wondered where God could be found during a terrible war. And I began to realize that there were all kinds of questions that Delbert had never voiced in those Friday Bible studies. Where was God?

As I walked back from the Craftsbury Community Care Center to the manse, I looked up at the 4 AM October Vermont sky, and I could see Orion and the Pleiades staring back down. "Where was God?" Delbert had asked, and a voice from the sky seemed to ask in return, "Can *you* bind the chains of the Pleiades, or loose the cords of Orion?"

As I said, the 38th chapter of the Book of Job contains some of the most beautiful poetry you can find in the Hebrew Bible, but is it enough to sustain us? Nearly all biblical scholars are agreed that it doesn't really answer Job's questions. But beyond that point, there's **not** a lot of agreement. One scholar lists eight different interpretations of God's response to Job.[27] Can you imagine trying to summarize all eight of those interpretations this morning? We'd be here for three hours. And then again, the Broncos have a BYE this week. So, if you had to pick a Sunday for a three-hour sermon, maybe today would be it. But I promise that I'm not going to preach for three hours.

And at the very end of God's speech in these chapters, when

---

[27] Old Testament scholar Leo Perdue lists eight different possible ways to interpret God's response to Job, as summarized by Samuel Balentine, *Job* (Macon, Georgia: Smyth & Helwys Publishing, 2006), 628.

Job finally speaks, Job says that he's rendered silent. And maybe the wise preacher is rendered silent as well. Perhaps the best way to understand the 38th chapter of Job is not by listening to a sermon. Perhaps a trip to the mountains would be better, with an opportunity to gaze into the night sky far away from the city lights. And whatever problems you take with you to the mountains, the mountains seem huge enough to absorb them. Perhaps the mountains are too big to care.[28]

Does the mountain care if you continue in your job or not? Is the mountain concerned whether or not your adult children are having trouble making their way in the world, or not? Do the mountains care about your own deep, deep, questions of faith? And maybe there's a comfort in that, in putting our own problems in perspective, in realizing that creation—the universe—is much, much bigger than we can possibly imagine. And as we meditate on the God who is complex and beautiful and wondrous enough to have created everything we see, maybe there is some comfort in hearing that voice say, "I am God, and you are not."

And it also means that when people like Job's friends come up to us and are quick to say that our own suffering is the will of God, then we can also say, "Well, God is God, and you are not." If anyone tries to answer our deep questions of faith too neatly or too tidily, we can always say, "Well, God is God, and you are not."

---

[28] My thinking here owes a great deal to insights from Belden Lane, *The Solace of Fierce Landscapes* (New York: Oxford University Press, 1998).

Theologians will often talk about the transcendence of God, that God is beyond anything that we can think or imagine, and the immanence of God, that God is just as near as the sound of our own breath. The hymn that we're going to sing at the end of the service, "How Great Thou Art," is a hymn about the transcendence of God. In contrast, the hymn "In the Garden," with its familiar refrain, "He walks with me, and He talks with me," is a hymn about immanence. The 38th chapter of the Book of Job is transcendence with a capital T. But maybe there is an inkling of immanence as well.

Were you surprised a moment ago in the children's sermon when the voice out of the storm was a grandmother's voice? Well, I wonder if we can imagine the 38th chapter of Job this way:

Here is this wonderful and magnificent catalog of everything that has been created, and God is like the grandmother who has invited us into her living room, and we can see that every square inch of every wall is covered with pictures.[29] There's a giraffe, there's an elephant. There's an octopus, there's a snail. And God, like a proud grandmother, shows off each and every picture. At one point God comes to a picture of a mosquito and says, *"Here's a mosquito. I know that all the time people question why I would have ever created a mosquito, but here it is. Even*

---

[29] This thought experiment was inspired by one of my former teachers. See William P. Brown, "Job's Place in Creation" in *The Seven Pillars of Creation: The Bible, Science, and the Ecology of Wonder* (New York: Oxford University Press, 2010), 130-131.

the mosquito is a part of the creation and has a place on the wall."

And those great monsters, Leviathan and Behemoth, are there, too. In the ancient world Leviathan and Behemoth symbolized all the forces of chaos, but in God's living room we can see Leviathan swimming around in a goldfish bowl and Behemoth running around in a hamster wheel.[30]

And here's the thing. If every creature in creation has its own picture, its own honored place on God's living room wall, then don't you know that there are also pictures of you and me?

---

[30] Thomas G. Long speaks of Leviathan and Behemoth as monsters that embodied the forces of chaos, but here they are creatures of God's creation, as if Leviathan were a pet sparrow. See Thomas G. Long, *What Shall We Say?: Evil, Suffering, and the Crisis of Faith* (Grand Rapids: Wm. B. Eerdmans, 2011), 108.

Risking a New Beginning

Westminster Presbyterian Church
Westminster, Colorado
October 28, 2012

Then Job answered the LORD*: "I know that you can do all things, and that no purpose of yours can be thwarted. Who is this that hides counsel without knowledge?' Therefore, I have uttered what I did not understand, things too wonderful for me, which I did not know. 'Hear, and I will speak; I will question you, and you declare to me.' I had heard of you by the hearing of the ear, but now my eye sees you; therefore, I despise myself, and repent in dust and ashes."*

After the LORD *had spoken these words to Job, the* LORD *said to Eliphaz the Temanite: "My wrath is kindled against you and against your two friends; for you have not spoken of me what is right, as my servant Job has.*

—Job 42:1-7

I am thinking of my favorite Warner Brothers Bugs Bunny cartoon. It was called "What's Opera, Doc?" Do you remember that one? Elmer Fudd and Bugs Bunny sang tunes from the operas of Wagner. Elmer Fudd, dressed as the demigod Siegfried, vowed that he was going to "kill the wabbit." When Bugs Bunny asked him how he was going to kill the wabbit, Elmer Fudd declared that he would kill the "wabbit" with his "spear and magic helmet." And then Bugs

Bunny, in obvious disguise, appeared as Brünnhilde, and Elmer Fudd fell in love. But then the little Viking hat fell off Bugs's head, and when Elmer Fudd saw Bugs's ears, he realized that Brünnhilde was actually the wabbit! In a rage, Elmer Fudd went to the top of the mountain where he used his magic helmet to conjure up terrible thunder and lightning. And then the wabbit was dead. Immediately, Elmer Fudd showed remorse. Tearfully, he picked up Bugs's lifeless body and carried it away in his arms. And then, in a little wink to the audience, Bugs Bunny lifted up his head and said, "Well, what did you expect in an opera, a happy ending?"

Well, what kind of ending do you expect to the Book of Job? A happy ending? I mean, really, Job has lost everything—his fortune, his entire family, his health. He sits on top of an ash heap with no consolation except friends who try to convince him that he must have done something wrong. Do we really expect a happy ending?

Several people have noticed how that the Book of Job has prose at the very beginning and at the end. And in the middle are these long chapters of beautiful poetry, asking the deep questions of faith, and then suddenly, there's a happy ending?!? It's as if Hollywood were trying to write the ending to the Book of Job. It would be as bad as trying to put a happy ending onto Hamlet or King Lear or Romeo and Juliet.

A lot of people read through the Book of Job, and they're not quite sure if this happy ending rings true. There are a number of scholars, including Sam Balentine, and others, who think that maybe the original story of Job was much shorter. Perhaps originally Job was a short story about a man who lost everything, who refused to curse God or to make any false confessions about his own wrongdoing, and then whose fortunes were restored. But perhaps even in ancient times such an abruptly happy ending didn't quite ring true, which is why we now have the very long middle section of poetry in which Job wrestles with the deep questions of faith.[31]

It also turns out that chapter 42 is not quite as neat and tidy an ending as it first appears. After God has been speaking, Job says, "I have heard of you by the hearing of the ear and now my eye sees you, therefore I despise myself and repent in dust and ashes." That's how the New Revised Standard Version puts it. It seems to have Job saying that maybe it wasn't so wise for him to question God through all those long chapters, and now Job is simply going to be quiet.

But that may or may not be the right translation. Stephen Mitchell translates it this way, "I have heard of you with my ears but now my eyes have seen you so therefore I will be quiet and comforted that I am dust." In other words, Job is saying that "I am comforted that I am a human being, who lives in the shadow of a great and wonderful God, even though there are many mysteries that I don't understand."[32] It might mean

---

[31] Samuel Balentine, *Job* (Macon, Georgia: Smyth & Helwys Publishing, 2006), 14.

[32] For a comparison of the NRSV translation and Stephen Mitchell's translation, see Thomas G. Long, *What Shall We Say?: Evil, Suffering, and the*

something like that.

And then a little bit later, Job prays for his friends, and we are left to assume that Job is offering an intercession for his friends, but Sam Balentine even wonders about that. It doesn't say what Job says in his prayers. Maybe Job is meekly praying that his friends be forgiven. But, after all those chapters of arguing and wrestling with God, do we really think that Job is going to be so quiet now? Maybe when Job prays this time he is still praying an honest, anguished prayer to God, saying, "Thank you for the vindication, thank you for at long last telling my friends that I have done nothing wrong. But I still don't understand why I've been made to suffer." Who knows what Job prays for when he prays?[33]

And then Job's fortunes are restored. Maybe it's because Job prayed for a restoration of his fortune, but the text doesn't actually say that. We're left to assume that the restoration of Job's fortune is just as mysterious as the loss of the fortune in the first place. We don't know why Job gets his fortune back. And it says he got double his fortune back. In the Book of Exodus, if a thief steals livestock, he's obligated to return to the person he stole from twice what he stole. Is this an admission on God's part that Job has not been treated right?

Crisis of Faith (Grand Rapids: Wm. B. Eerdmans Publishing Company, 2011), 109-110.

[33]See Samuel Balentine, "My Servant Job Shall Pray for You," *Theology Today*, January 1, 2002.

Is this why Job's fortunes are doubled?[34] We don't know.

So even this neat, tidy, happy ending of chapter 42 is full of mysteries and not quite as neat and tidy as we might have supposed. And then Job has seven sons and three daughters, he gets to see four generations, and he dies old and full of days. This is the kind of happy ending that makes us more than a little bit suspicious.

But here's the thing. When the first child was born, Job doesn't yet know that there are going to be nine more children. He doesn't yet know that he's going to get to see four generations. He doesn't yet know that he's going to die old and full of days. All he knows is that a child has been born. And he does not know what the future holds for that child. After all, all of his other children died. What a scary and frightening thing to bring another child into the world, considering everything that has already happened to Job.

But then a second child is born. And Job doesn't know what will happen to that child. And then a third child is born, and Job doesn't yet know what will happen to any of these new children. He doesn't know what will happen in his own life. And a fourth child is born, and Job still does not know the future.

But each time a child is born, Job is willing to risk a new

---

[34] Exodus 22:4. See comments by Samuel Balentine, *Job*, 715-717.

beginning.[35] Even though he had lost his children before, even though he had lost his health and all of his fortune, Job is willing to risk a new beginning with each new child.

The Russian novelist Dostoevsky once said that the real miracle of the Book of Job is not that Job got a new family or that his fortunes were doubled. The real miracle in the Book of Job is that Job was able to love and to embrace his new family, especially after everything that he had lost, especially after the tremendous heartbreak that he suffered earlier. In spite of everything, Job is able to risk a new beginning.

So what does Job pray for when he prays? I think he prays for himself. I think he continues to argue with and to wrestle with God, but each time he comes back to pray some more. I think that Job does pray for his friends. I think that he prays for his new family. He prays for his new life, and he prays for the courage to begin again and again and again.

And he prays for us. He prays for each one here for that same courage to begin again no matter what heartaches we've experienced. He prays for those parents that are worried about their adult children and how they are making their way in the world. He prays for a community that is torn apart by the murder of a ten-year-old girl and how a seventeen-year-old could be implicated in such a terrible crime. He prays for those who are worried about their country and its politics. He prays

---

[35] I'm in debt to preacher and writer Martin Copenhaver for the idea of "Risking a Happy Ending," which was also the title to his article on Job 42, which appeared in *The Christian Century*, October 12, 1994.

for those who are worried about the future of their church. And for all of us, Job prays that we would have the courage to risk a new beginning.

Risking a New Beginning

Jack Cabaness

Sermons Rewritten on Saturday in Response to Friday's News

Risking a New Beginning

Why Did Jesus Have to Die?

Katonah Presbyterian Church
Katonah, New York
June 28, 2015

For while we were still weak, at the right time Christ died for the ungodly. Indeed, rarely will anyone die for a righteous person—though perhaps for a good person someone might actually dare to die. But God proves his love for us in that while we still were sinners Christ died for us. Much more surely then, now that we have been justified by his blood, will we be saved through him from the wrath of God. For if while we were enemies, we were reconciled to God through the death of his Son, much more surely, having been reconciled, will we be saved by his life. But more than that, we even boast in God through our Lord Jesus Christ, through whom we have now received reconciliation.

—Romans 5:6-11

Beloved, let us love one another, because love is from God; everyone who loves is born of God and knows God. Whoever does not love does not know God, for God is love. God's love was revealed among us in this way: God sent his only Son into the world so that we might live through him. In this is love, not that we loved God but that he loved us and sent his Son to be the atoning sacrifice for our sins. Beloved, since God loved us so much, we also ought to love one another.

—1 John 4:7-11

This morning we continue our sermon series Questions from the Floor. All of our sermons this summer are based on questions that you submitted. Today's question is

Why did Jesus have to die for our sins? Why didn't God just love us enough to forgive us without Jesus having to die?

At the beginning, I need to acknowledge my reliance on two sources.

The first is a chapter from a book by the late Shirley C. Guthrie, Jr., who taught theology at Columbia Seminary in Georgia and whose book generations of Presbyterian ministers have used to cram for their theology ordination exam.

The second source is a book by my college classmate and well-known author in Emergent Church circles Tony Jones, which is entitled *Did God Kill Jesus? Searching for Love in History's Most Famous Execution*.

Imagine the scene. A young boy goes to a revival meeting. He had grown up in a Christian home and in the church, but he heard something that night he had never heard before.

The preacher held up a dirty glass. "See this glass? That's you. Filthy, stained with sin, inside and outside." He picked up a hammer. "This hammer is the righteousness of God. It is the instrument of God's wrath against sinners. God's justice can be satisfied only by punishing and destroying people whose lives are filled with vileness and corruption."

The preacher put the glass on the pulpit and slowly, deliberately drew back the hammer, took deadly aim, and with all his might let the blow fall.

But a miracle happened!

At the last moment, he covered the glass with a pan. The hammer struck with a crash that echoed through the hushed church. He held up the untouched glass with one hand and the mangled pan with the other.

Then the preacher said, "Jesus Christ died for your sins. He took the punishment that ought to have fallen on you. He satisfied the righteousness of God so that you might go free if you believe in him."

When the boy went to bed that night, he could not sleep. Meditating on what he had seen and heard, he decided that he was terribly afraid of God. But could he love such a God? He could love Jesus who had sacrificed himself for him. But how could he love a God who wanted to "get" everyone and was only kept from doing it because Jesus got in the way? The thought crossed the boy's mind that he could only hate such a hammer-swinging God who had to be bought off at such a terrible price. But he quickly dismissed the thought. That very God might read his mind and punish him.[36]

The question for us this morning is can we think about the atonement in such a way that helps us to love both God and Jesus? Can we think about what happened on Calvary long ago in a way that makes it clear that God is for us and not against us?

Listen again to the two scripture readings that were shared this morning. From Romans 5, "But God proves his *love* for us in that while we still were sinners Christ died for us." And from First John 4, "God's *love* was revealed among us in this way: God sent his only Son

---

[36] Illustration from Shirley C. Guthrie, Jr., *Christian Doctrine* (Louisville: Westminster/John Knox Press, 1994), 250-251.

into the world so that we might live through him. In this is love, not that we loved God but that he loved us and sent his Son to be the atoning sacrifice for our sins. Beloved, since God loved us so much, we also ought to love one another."

It's about Love. Love Wins. And God is the one who loves us, and God loves us every bit as much as Jesus loves us. Whatever theory best helps you understand the atonement, make sure that it enables you to sense and experience the love of God.

According to Shirley Guthrie there are at least four main perspectives that emerge from the New Testament to interpret the meaning of the death of Jesus.

The first is redemption. This is the financial image. Imagine a slave market. People have lost their freedom and are being sold into slavery. But someone steps forward and pays the ransom, the price for the purchase of all the slaves. The price is high. His life for ours. But Jesus on the cross pays the price of our redemption and sets us free.

The second perspective draws upon the imagery of war. Jesus is the liberator. A terrible cosmic battle is being waged between God and Satan. Satan has stolen humanity from the Kingdom of God and carried it to the realm of darkness. At the cross, Satan takes the prisoner, Jesus, captive and wins the battle of death, but it's a temporary victory. On Easter morning, Jesus the prisoner becomes Jesus the liberator and wins the final victory, delivering us from death to life.

The third explanation has to do with sacrifice. To quote the Gospel of John, "Jesus is the Lamb of God who takes away the sins of the world." (John 1:29). All of us stand guilty before God, deserving punishment. But a priest comes forward who makes a sacrifice to atone for the peoples' sins. The lamb is slain, reconciling humanity to God.

The final perspective comes from the language of the courtroom. God is a righteous judge, who sits behind the bench, with humanity standing in the dock as the accused. The case is argued, and humanity is found guilty, receiving a sentence of death. But a righteous and good person comes forward and offers himself as a substitute for the guilty, taking their punishment upon himself even though he has done nothing wrong.

Whichever perspective resonates with us the most, we should make sure that we interpret each of these images in a way that makes it clear that God loves us just as much as Jesus loves us and in a way that makes it clear that God is for us and not against us.

For example, the financial model does not mean that God is bought off by Jesus.

It means that we are purchased for God. God purchases for us the gift of a new life, much like the bishop in *Les Misérables* gives to Jean Valjean as a gift the very silver that Jean Valjean had tried to steal from the bishop. And the Bishop tells Jean Valjean to use the gift of the silver to make for himself a new life. "I have bought your life for God," the bishop tells him.

Likewise, with the sacrificial image, we should interpret that image in such a way that God is for us and not against us. In the ancient world, many people believed that when the gods were angry at humanity, the gods had to appeased with sacrifice. But what if it's not God that needs to be appeased, but it's humanity that needs to see and understand that violence only begets violence and that violence is never redemptive?

René Girard studied and taught world religions and ancient myths. He later converted to Christianity largely because of the theology of the cross. My college classmate Tony Jones summarizes Girard's view in this way: When we look at Jesus hanging on the cross, we are looking in a mirror. God is reflecting back to us the outcome of our systems of rivalry, sacrifice, and violence. Jesus' death shows conclusively that these systems are bankrupt, that they do not assuage guilt, and that they do not minimize violence. Jesus, as the ultimate innocent victim, is the final sacrifice because he reveals the fiction behind the entire enterprise of sacrifice.[37]

Girard draws upon the story of Joseph and his brothers in the Book of Genesis. Joseph's brothers try to kill him but decide to sell him into slavery instead. Joseph eventually rises from a slave to being second in power only to the Pharaoh. Many years later, when Joseph's brothers come to Egypt because there is famine in their land, Joseph does not seek revenge against his brothers. He does toy with them for several chapters, but he doesn't seek revenge and he doesn't try to have them killed. Tearfully, Joseph reveals himself to his brothers and tells them who he is. And Joseph tells them, what you intended for evil, God intended for good.

Girard's view of the crucifixion is similar. What humanity intended for evil in killing Jesus, God intended for good. We see an example of this in President Obama's moving eulogy on Friday for the Rev. Clementa Pinckney. In that speech, the President reflected on the shooter's announced motive of hoping to start a race war. The

---

[37] from Tony Jones, *Did God Kill Jesus?: Looking for Love in History's Most Famous Execution* (New York: HarperOne, 2015), see especially chapter 16.

President described that as …

> An act that [the shooter] imagined would incite fear and recrimination; violence and suspicion. An act that he presumed would deepen divisions that trace back to our nation's original sin.
>
> Oh, but God works in mysterious ways. (Applause.) God has different ideas. (Applause.)
>
> He didn't know he was being used by God. (Applause.) Blinded by hatred, the alleged killer could not see the grace surrounding Reverend Pinckney and that Bible study group — the light of love that shone as they opened the church doors and invited a stranger to join in their prayer circle. The alleged killer could have never anticipated the way the families of the fallen would respond when they saw him in court — in the midst of unspeakable grief, with words of forgiveness. He couldn't imagine that. (Applause.)
>
> The alleged killer could not imagine how the city of Charleston, how the state of South Carolina, how the United States of America would respond — not merely with revulsion at his evil act, but with big-hearted generosity and, more importantly, with a thoughtful introspection and self-examination that we so rarely see in public life.[38]

Truly, what the shooter intended for evil, God redirected for good.

Why did Jesus have to die? Why couldn't God have just forgiven us

---

[38] Transcript of President Obama's Eulogy of Rev. Pinckney from Vox.com, retrieved June 27, 2015

without Jesus having to die? In the quote that is printed on the cover of your bulletin, Shirley Guthrie responds by saying that God loves us and cares for us too much to dismiss our sin and guilt with a flippant "It doesn't matter." God wanted to stand with us in the loneliness and alienation we bring on ourselves when we separate ourselves from God and other people. Because it is just when God comes to our side in our loneliness, alienation, and guilt that they are overcome.[39]

In his book, my college classmate Tony Jones takes this a step further and says that in the cross God identifies with us so completely that when Jesus cries out on the cross, "My God, My God, why have you forsaken me?" that even God suddenly realizes what it is like to feel abandoned by God.[40]

[Pause]

And at the end of the day, contemplating the cross is more of a matter of the heart than of the head. And I'm not talking about the emotional manipulation of a preacher who points the finger and says that because of your sin Jesus died a horrific death. No. Instead, I'm talking about journeying to the cross in our hearts with honesty and authenticity. In the words of the old spiritual, "Were you there when they crucified my Lord? Sometimes it makes me want to tremble." A theory of the atonement is not likely to make us tremble. A journey to the cross will.

I've had the good fortune to see the traditional site of the crucifixion in the Church of the Holy Sepulcher in Jerusalem, but in truth my

---

[39] Guthrie, 260.

[40] Jones, chapter 19.

real journey to the cross took place in a chapel service at Union Seminary in Richmond, Virginia. It was a year after my father had died of pancreatic cancer. My mother was facing her own significant health issues, and I was an only child in my mid-twenties and feeling lonely and more than a little overwhelmed. In the chapel service, we sang

> *What Wondrous Love is this, o my soul, o my soul,*
> *What wondrous love is this, o my soul*
> *What wondrous love is this that caused the Lord of Bliss*
> *to bear the heavy cross for my soul.*

And I had this sense that all the fear, loneliness, helplessness, hopelessness, brokenness, and all the other heavy things were being borne by Jesus on the cross. And the tears started flowing and they wouldn't stop.

—All of you who grieve.

—All of you who mourn the loss of life or the end of a marriage.

—All of you who mourn the loss of a dream.

—All of you who are living with a terminal illness.

—All of you who deeply regret something that you have done that you wish more than anything that you could undo.

—All of you who worry about an adult child making his or her way in the world.

Jesus on the cross identifies with you in all of your struggles and even knows what it's like to cry in desperation, "My God, My God, why have you forsaken me?"

God experienced humanity fully in the Cross of Christ. And the hope is this:

> that just as God experienced humanity fully in dying a real human death—even a brutal human death—so we, too, can experience new life with God in the resurrection.

As I stood there in the chapel service with tears streaming down my face, those around me sang the third stanza, even as my heart was too full to sing myself. Those around me sang

> *And when from death I'm free, I'll sing on, I'll sing on,*
> *and when from death I'm free, I'll sing on*
> *And when from death I'm free I'll sing and joyful be.*
> *And through eternity I'll sing on, I'll sing on,*
> *and through eternity, I'll sing on.*

Working Through the Unimaginable

Katonah Presbyterian Church
Katonah, New York
July 10, 2016

If then there is any encouragement in Christ, any consolation from love, any sharing in the Spirit, any compassion and sympathy, make my joy complete: be of the same mind, having the same love, being in full accord and of one mind. Do nothing from selfish ambition or conceit, but in humility regard others as better than yourselves. Let each of you look not to your own interests, but to the interests of others. Let the same mind be in you that was in Christ Jesus, who, though he was in the form of God, did not regard equality with God as something to be exploited, but emptied himself, taking the form of a slave, being born in human likeness. And being found in human form, he humbled himself and became obedient to the point of death—even death on a cross. Therefore, God also highly exalted him and gave him the name that is above every name, so that at the name of Jesus every knee should bend, in heaven and on earth and under the earth, and every tongue should confess that Jesus Christ is Lord, to the glory of God the Father.

—Philippians 2:1-11

There's a poignant and moving scene in the Broadway musical *Hamilton*. It takes place after the tragic death of Alexander and Eliza Hamilton's oldest son Philip, who died in a gun duel, eerily foreshadowing Alexander's own death in a duel with Aaron Burr.

In his grief, Alexander Hamilton walks the streets of New York City, and the ensemble cast sings

> *If you see him in the street, walking by himself, talking to himself, have pity. He is working through the unimaginable.*

And then the men sing

> *his hair has gone grey, he passes every day, they say he walks the length of the city. He is working through the unimaginable.*

I feel that's where we are as a nation after this last week. We are working through the unimaginable.

On Tuesday, a graphic video showed the killing of an African-American man, Alton Sterling, by police in Baton Rouge.

On Wednesday, police fatally shot another man, Philando Castile, after pulling him over for a broken taillight outside of St. Paul, and the horrifying incident was broadcast on Facebook Live by Castile's girlfriend.

Then, the next evening, came the vicious murder of five Dallas police officers—Brent Thompson, Patrick Zamarripa, Michael Krol, Michael Smith, and Lorne Ahrens. The five were patrolling what had been a peaceful protest up until that moment.

All that was last week. And the grief and the rage are worldwide.

One week ago today, on Sunday, July 3rd, a suicide bombing in Baghdad, Iraq killed an estimated 250 people, making it the deadliest attack in Iraq in a decade. And before last week there was the airport shooting and bombing in Istanbul, Turkey on June 28th that left 48 dead, and before that there was the shooting at the Pulse nightclub in Orlando, Florida in the early morning hours of June 12th that left 50 dead.

As one of the characters in Hamilton sings,

> *There are moments that the words don't reach. There is suffering too terrible to name, You hold your child as tight as you can. And push away the unimaginable.*

And maybe that's the first thing that any honest sermon offered on this particular Sunday should say. There are moments when the words don't reach. There are moments when all of us are trying to work through the unimaginable.

So, what do we say as people of faith? What can we say?

I think that we should begin from a place of humility. When our own words fail us, we can strive to listen, listening particularly to the voices of those who are the most vulnerable, those who are grieving, angry, and afraid.

One of the most powerful lessons in humility I know comes from the second chapter of Philippians. The Apostle Paul is in prison, not knowing whether he will ever get out alive. He urges the Philippians to have the same attitude in them that was also in Christ, and then he breaks out into song.

For nearly a hundred years the consensus among New Testament scholars has been that Philippians 2:6-11 is a hymn.

The syntax and the cadence suddenly shift from prose to poetry, and most scholars do believe that Paul is quoting a hymn, perhaps even a hymn that he wrote.

Paul sings about Christ Jesus,

> *Who, though he was in the form of God, did not regard equality with God as something to be exploited, but emptied himself, taking the form of a slave, being born in human likeness.*
>
> *And being found in human form, he humbled himself and became obedient to the point of death—even death on a cross.*

That little phrase, even death on a cross, is a phrase that Paul added. It breaks up the meter of the poem, and in the words of one commentator, indicates that Paul has chosen theology over poetry.[41]

Instead of offering glib answers to the question of human suffering and the horror of human evil, Paul gives us a picture of Jesus giving up the privilege of heaven to embrace an earthly life in service to others, even when that service to others puts his own life in jeopardy.

Our model of Jesus is a Jesus who gives up privilege in order to stand in solidarity with those who are suffering, with those who are grieving, with those who are angry, and with those who are afraid. What does that say to us in the context of the

---

[41] Fred Craddock, *Philippians,* Interpretation: A Biblical Commentary for Teaching and Preaching (Atlanta: John Knox Press, 1985), 39.

debate about white privilege? At the very least, might it motivate us to listen, to seek first to understand, and then to be understood, in the famous words of St. Francis.

My friend Matt Hackworth once worked as a reporter for National Public Radio. On Friday he wrote,

> When I was a young reporter, I spent enough time riding with officers in police cars in the dark of night to understand what it's like for them to face fear and uncertainty.
>
> I have also spent considerable time in courts, prisons, and the social justice movement to know there is certainly bias in our criminal system. I know wonderful people who wear a badge, and other wonderful people who fear the badge.
>
> My prayer is wonderful people on both sides can find a way forward that respects both life and law, so that justice might be righteous and abundant, and these tragic shootings might not be in vain. (from a Facebook post, July 8, 2016).

Following Christ's example, we can offer a listening ear and a willingness to stand in solidarity with those who have been the most impacted by these recent tragic events.

Ashley Ann Masters is a Presbyterian minister who works as a chaplain in a children's hospital in Chicago. On Friday she put on her clergy collar and walked into a police station on the South side of Chicago, and she said,

> "Thank you for showing up to work. I'm sorry for how broken so many systems and hearts are. How are you? Because if anyone deserves gratitude for putting on pants and going to work today, it's every skin color wearing blue."

Ashely-Anne was the only white person in the room. One officer said, "A lot about this week is shocking, and you walking in here is up there." (from a Facebook post, July 8, 2016).

Perhaps it was shocking, but that's what happens when people begin to imitate Christ's example of humility. We can begin with our own loved ones and colleagues, taking the time to check in on those for whom the events of the past week have been particularly distressing. We can provide space in our worship this morning for the grief and lament. As time moves on, we can be more intentional about our acts of humble service.

In the words of Brian McLaren, here's what will happen to you if you listen to the Spirit.

> You will be in a public place. You will see a person who, by their dress or language or mannerisms, is clearly from another religion, another culture, another social class. That person will be uncomfortable or in need. And you will feel the Spirit inspiring a question

> within you. "If I were in their shoes—in an unfamiliar or uncomfortable environment, what would I want someone to do for me?" And you will move toward them. You will overcome differences in language or culture. Your kind eyes and warm smile and gentle presence will speak a universal language of neighborliness. And in that moment, they will feel that God is real, for God's Spirit is alive in you.[42]

And in humility, let us admit that this spirit of humility is not limited to Christian circles. On Wednesday, Sunni and Shiite Muslims in Iraq held a joint prayer vigil in Baghdad in remembrance of the victims of Sunday's deadly car bombing and in a joint show of defiance against ISIS.

Indeed, Christians are not the only ones who practice humility, but when we practice humility, we do so because we are following Christ's example.

The sermon I had originally written for this morning included many more examples of humble service, but I am thinking that I should wait and perhaps share them next week when our sermon topic will be the Spirit Conspiracy.

I'm still inclined to think that today our most important work is listening and solidarity.

---

[42] Brian D. McLaren, *We Make the Road by Walking* (New York: Jericho Books, 2014), 233.

In the musical *Hamilton*, Alexander's sister-in-law Angelica is the one who sings that there is a **suffering** too **terrible** to name. But near the end of the song, she also sings that there is a **grace** too **powerful** to name. It is a grace that makes forgiveness and reconciliation possible.

In the song that Paul sings, Paul names that grace anyway. For the Christian, the name of that grace is Jesus.

Last Things—Sermons on Ultimate Hopes

Judgment Day

Katonah Presbyterian Church
Katonah, New York
August 7, 2016

O sing to the LORD a new song, for he has done marvelous things.

His right hand and his holy arm have gotten him victory. The LORD has made known his victory; he has revealed his vindication in the sight of the nations.

He has remembered his steadfast love and faithfulness to the house of Israel.

All the ends of the earth have seen the victory of our God.

Make a joyful noise to the LORD, all the earth;

break forth into joyous song and sing praises.

Sing praises to the LORD with the lyre, with the lyre and the sound of melody. With trumpets and the sound of the horn make a joyful noise before the King, the LORD. Let the sea roar, and all that fills it; the world and those who live in it. Let the floods clap their hands;

let the hills sing together for joy at the presence of the LORD for he is coming to judge the earth.

He will judge the world with righteousness, and the peoples with equity.

—Psalm 98

For we are God's servants, working together; you are God's field, God's building. According to the grace of God given to me, like a skilled master builder I laid a foundation, and someone else is building on it. Each builder must choose with care how to build on it. For no one can lay any foundation other than the one that has been laid; that foundation is Jesus Christ. Now if anyone builds on the foundation with gold, silver, precious stones, wood, hay, straw—the work of each builder will become visible, for the Day will disclose it, because it will be revealed with fire, and the fire will test what sort of work each has done. If what has been built on the foundation survives, the builder will receive a reward. If the work is burned up, the builder will suffer loss; the builder will be saved, but only as through fire.

—1 Corinthians 3:9-15

In traditional depictions of the Last Judgment, the saved are gathered on the right side of the throne (preacher gestures toward the right), and the condemned are gathered on the left side (preacher gestures toward the left). In the interests of fairness, I should do the same illustration facing the opposite direction, so that all of you can now be on the saved side! (preacher gestures toward those who are now on the preacher's right, who were formerly on the left). I don't want to discriminate arbitrarily against any of our worshippers this morning!

And yet our traditional images of judgment are inherently discriminatory. The saved are on one side, and the condemned on the other. In many of the famous paintings of the Last Judgment, including Michelangelo's in the Sistine Chapel, the faces of the condemned are filled with anguish as devils and demons reach out to drag them into the nether reaches of Hell, and meanwhile, the faces of those on the right, who are slowly ascending to Heaven, almost seem to take satisfaction in the torment of the condemned. Several art historians allege that Michelangelo even depicted the faces of some of his most ardent critics in the faces of those who were being condemned as part of his own revenge.

Perhaps in reaction to such vengeful understandings of the Last Judgment, mainline Protestants have had a tendency to deemphasize the symbol of the Last Judgment altogether. When was the last time you heard a sermon about the Last Judgment in a Presbyterian Church? In all honesty, I've probably only preached about it two or three times myself, including today's sermon, and usually when I was doing a sermon series on the Apostles' Creed. On those occasions I would try to articulate what we mean when we say that Christ will come again to judge the living and the dead. And I would try to say that the doctrine of the Last Judgment is meant to give us hope. It gives us hope that at long last God will judge, or adjust, everything that is wrong with our world. It gives us hope that the imperfect and incomplete justice we experience in this world will not have the last word.

In the words of Christian author Brian McLaren,

> people of faith have trusted that God can continue to set things right on the other side of the threshold of death. Through the idea of the final judgment, we have dared to hope that somehow, beyond what we see in history, restorative judgment could have the last word.[43]

Even one of the most frightening images of judgment, the image of fire, is best understood not as an instrument of torture but as an instrument of purification. Perhaps you remember some of the lines from Handel's Messiah.

An alto sings verses from the book of Malachi ...

> *But who may abide the day of his coming?*
>
> *And who shall stand when he appeareth? For he is like a refiner's fire.*

And then the chorus sings ....

> *And he shall purify the sons of Levi,*
>
> *That they may offer unto the Lord an offering in righteousness.*

All those corrupt temple priests, all those corrupt religious leaders—the sons of Levi—will be purified so that their service

---

[43] Brian D. McLaren, *We Make the Road by Walking* (New York: Jericho Books, 2014), 245.

will be an honorable offering in righteousness, and not one marred by hypocrisy. That's the hope that the Prophet Malachi expressed. Likewise, in First Corinthians, the Apostle Paul speaks of a purifying fire. According to Paul, all of us are constructing together a building. If we use shoddy materials, then they will get burned away in the fire. But if we use gold, silver, and precious stones, then they won't get consumed in the fire.

So, if some of us have constructed our lives like a shoddy builder, using worthless materials, there won't be much of our life's story left. We will survive, but only as one who survives the fire, in Paul's words. Indeed, we will experience the purification of judgment as loss, regret, and remorse. Others of us will be surprised that thousands of deeds of kindness that we had long forgotten will have been remembered by God.[44]

Does this mean that all of us will be saved, even if some of us will have more of our life's work burned up than others?

Those who answer this question with a firm "no" point to judgment scenes in the Gospel of Matthew or in the Book of Revelation which suggest that there are eternal rewards and eternal punishments, while those who answer this question with a confident "yes" point to Jesus' statement in John 12 that "he will draw all people to himself" or to Paul's statement near

---

[44] McLaren, 246-247.

the end of Romans 11 when Paul speaks about God having mercy on all.

However, we might approach this question theologically and how ever we might answer this question theologically, I do believe that our attitude should be one of hope. In the words of the Second Helvetic Confession, written in 1536, we should not unduly speculate about who is saved and who is not, but we should maintain a good hope for all. I love that. "We should maintain a good hope for all." Keep in mind that these are not liberal-minded Protestants of the 21st century. These were 16th century, first-generation Calvinists who firmly believed in double predestination, and yet they beckon us to "maintain a good hope for all."

Don't be like the gleeful faces in Michelangelo's painting taking delight in the torments of the condemned. Instead, maintain a good hope for all.

And yet, this hope, this understanding of restorative judgment absolutely changes the way we live before we die. In McLaren's words,

> it makes you eager to use your wealth to make others rich, not to hoard it. It inspires you to use your power to empower others, not to advance yourself. [It motivates you to work toward a more just society for everyone.]

And this hope also changes the way we see trials and difficulties in this life. If we see trials and difficulties

> not as punishment for our wrongs, but as a refining fire to strengthen and purify us, trials become our friends, not our enemies. So, in this light, delay is like a fire that burns away our impatience. Annoyances are like flames that burn away our selfishness.
>
> The demands of duty are like degrees of heat that burn away our laziness. The unkind words and deeds of others are like a furnace in which our character is tempered, until we learn to bless, not curse, in response.
>
> If we believe in judgment, in God's great setting things right, we won't live in fear.[45]

We will join God in God's pursuit of justice.

Preacher and writer Tom Long tells a story about an incident that took place many years ago on a cool September night at the old Yankee stadium. It's a wonderful baseball story, but in my view, it's also a parable about the Judgment. A foul ball was hit into the lower left field stands. It was headed right toward a boy of about nine who had obviously come to the game hoping that he might catch a foul ball. He had a pair of cheap binoculars around his neck and was wearing an oversized Yankees cap and a small Little League glove which had the

---

[45] McLaren, 247.

hardly-broken-in look of a mitt worn by a kid you let play right field in the late innings of hopeless games.

The foul ball was arching directly toward this boy's outstretched hand. But suddenly, a man of about thirty-five wearing an expensive knit shirt and horn-rimmed glasses reached over the boy, jostling him aside, and caught the ball. In the jostle, the man with the horn-rimmed glasses broke the young boy's plastic binoculars and the boy's heart.

Everybody in the left field stands had seen this, and, after a second or two of stunned silence, someone shouted, "Hey! Give the kid the ball!"

A couple of rows joined in unison: "Give the kid the ball!"

Horn Rims shook his head and put the ball in his pocket.

That inflamed the whole left field crowd, and with one voice they took up the chant, "Give the kid the ball!"

The chant spread to the center field stands, then to right field, until the whole outfield including people who did not even know the story, were shouting, "Give the kid the ball!"

Players began to glance up from the field to the stands to see what was going on.

Horn Rims remained stubbornly firm.

Finally, a man got up out of his seat, walked over to Horn Rims and spoke some words patiently and gently to him. Horn Rims hesitated, then reached into his pocket and handed the ball to the kid.

"He gave the kid the ball!" someone exclaimed.

Then the whole stands thundered, "He gave the kid the ball!" Applause rippled around the stadium.

Then an even more strange thing began to happen. When another foul ball landed in the left field stands, the man who caught it walked over to Horn Rims and gave it to him. Horn Rims looked incredulous, but he thanked him and took the ball.

Then there was another foul ball. This one was caught by a man in a muscle shirt, who turned and tossed the ball to the kid, who, to everyone's surprise and delight, caught it. Now the kid had two foul balls, and the stands erupted in enthusiastic applause.[46]

That scene that day in the old Yankee stadium may have more in common with the Last Judgment than Michelangelo's famous painting. It certainly has more in common with the imagery of Psalm 98, which Jim read a few minutes ago.

To all those cheering and chanting voices in the stadium, Psalm 98 adds

---

[46] Story told by Thomas G. Long, *Whispering the Lyrics* (Lima, Ohio: CSS Publishing, 1995), 132-133.

> *Let the sea roar, and all that fills it;*
>
> *The world, and those who live in it. Let the floods clap their hands;*
>
> *Let the hills sing together for joy at the presence of the Lord, for he is coming to judge the earth.*

The judgment of the Lord is cause for celebration. All of creation is shouting for joy, because at long last God is coming to judge, to make right everything that is wrong with the world.

From Dust to Life

First Presbyterian Church
Vallejo, California
December 8, 1996

Jesus said to her, "I am the resurrection and the life. Those who believe in me, even though they die, will live, and everyone who lives and believes in me will never die. Do you believe this?"

—John 11:25-26

"Where, O death, is your victory? Where, O death, is your sting?"

—I Corinthians 15:55

I believe ... in the resurrection of the body.

—The Apostles' Creed

Almost every morning I walk down to the 7-11 on the corner of Tennessee and Glenn streets for breakfast. Breakfast, by the way, is two Power Bars and a Mountain Dew. One morning, as I stood in line, I noticed the covers of Time and Newsweek, which were displayed side by side. The cover of Time had a picture of a young woman with the caption, "How science is searching for ways to keep us forever young." The cover of Newsweek had a picture of the late Cardinal Joseph Bernardin with the caption, "Teaching us how to die." Both covers are dated November 25, 1996. The Time article is about how medical researchers are trying to learn how to slow down or even stop the aging process. The Newsweek article is about struggling to accept death. Here were two very different approaches to dealing with the mystery of death, published by national news magazines on the same day.

The Apostles' Creed has its own answer for what happens to us when we die. Today we look at the next-to-last phrase: "the resurrection of the body." Some of us may wonder why that phrase is worded that way. Isn't it enough to say that we believe in the life everlasting or in the immortality of the soul? I'm not sure I could have answered that question even five years ago. I had grown up in the church and read through the Bible a few times (thanks in large part to my grandmother's challenge to read the Bible once through each year), but I'm not sure I could have easily distinguished the resurrection of the body from the immortality of the soul. One writer who helped me make this distinction was Presbyterian minister and novelist Frederick Buechner.

Buechner points out that the ancient Greeks believed in the immortality of the soul. The idea was that even though the body dies, the soul lives on and on. And, in fact, death was seen as a good thing, because the Greeks believed that souls were really better off without bodies, as if the human body were some sort of prison.[47]

---

[47] Frederick Buechner, "Immortality" and "Incarnation" in *Wishful Thinking: A Theological ABC* (San Francisco: HarperCollins, 1973, 1993), 49-52.

The Apostles' Creed reminds us that such escapist views are not really part of the Christian faith. When God made Adam, God slapped some mud together and breathed into Adam the breath of life, and Adam became a living soul. According to the Hebrew Scriptures, then, we are not souls that are forced to endure bodies the way a reluctant child might be forced to wear a coat and scarf on a wintery morning. Rather, we are soul and body mixed together. If we read Genesis carefully, we find that everything that God created is good, and that includes our bodies.

During this season of Advent, we are reminded of the verse in John that says, "the Word became flesh and dwelt among us." (John 1:14). The word flesh in that verse is the same word that is used in the Greek versions of the Apostles' Creed for the resurrection of the body. God is obviously not ashamed of bodies; in Jesus Christ God even became a human body. People who long for out-of-body experiences or for an escape from this world are, in the words of Frederick Buechner, trying to be "more spiritual than God."[48]

I suppose it's still easier for many people to believe in out-of-body experiences than it is for them to believe in resurrection. After all, we all know what happens to bodies when they die. They decay and become dust. And it's hard to believe that the process could ever be reversed. We wonder how resurrection

---

[48] Buechner, 52.

would work exactly. The Canadian rock group *Crash Test Dummies* has a song in which they ask, "And if your eye got poked out in this life, would it be up in heaven, waiting with your wife?"[49]

Even in New Testament times resurrection was a hard sale. True enough, the Pharisees believed in resurrection, but the Sadducees did not. (Which is why there were so sad, you see—a silly Sunday school pun, I'll admit, but an extremely effective mnemonic!) The Sadducees would annoy the Pharisees with elaborate hypotheticals such as: "Suppose a man went out walking one day and got eaten by a lion. Then the lion dies, and gets eaten by worms, and some of the worms crawl into the lake where they get eaten by little fish, and then the little fish get eaten by bigger fish, and then the bigger fish get caught and eaten by a fisherman. And then one day the fisherman dies. Well, in the resurrection, just who exactly gets resurrected? The first man? The lion? The worm? The little fish? The big fish? Or the fisherman?"[50]

To the Sadducees, the Crash Test Dummies, and to the Corinthians, the Apostle Paul had a direct response:

> [You] fool! What you sow does not come to life unless it dies. And as for what you sow, you do not sow the

---

[49] Song entitled, "God Shuffled His Feet," which is also the name of the album. Recorded by the Crash Test Dummies on the Arista label, 1993.

[50] Lecture by New Testament professor Paul Achtemeier, Union Theological Seminary in Virginia, Fall 1995.

> body that is to be, but a bare seed, perhaps of wheat or of some other grain. But God gives it a body as he has chosen, and to each kind of seed its own body. (1 Corinthians 15:35-38)

According to Paul, the Sadducees and the Crash Test Dummies miss the point because they don't realize that our resurrected bodies are going to be very different from our current bodies. However, there will also be some continuity—like the continuity between a seed and a plant.

In the Gospel of John, Jesus' response is even simpler and more to the point than Paul's. Jesus doesn't try to defend the resurrection; nor does he explain it by using colorful metaphors. Jesus simply says, "I am the resurrection and the life." Jesus makes the resurrection ***personal.***

One of the earliest memories of my father is that he loved to play albums on an old record player that he always referred to as the family jukebox. (It wasn't really a jukebox, of course, but for the first four years of my life, he had me fooled.) I especially remember how much he loved the Liza Minnelli version of Cabaret. He would hold me in his lap, whistling and tapping his foot in rhythm with the music, and he serenaded me with "Life is a cabaret, Ole Chum" so often that I began to wonder whether my name might be "Ole Chum" instead of Jack. In addition to being unsure about my name, I had no idea what a cabaret was, and I was left to assume that our family living room was a cabaret, because that's where my father always played his music.

My father died of cancer on March the sixth of this year. Life was not much of a cabaret for my Dad those last few months, and for most of this year life has not been much of a cabaret for my mom and me.

The promise of resurrection means that one day my Dad will get a new body but will still be my Dad. He'll have a new mouth to whistle with and a new foot to tap with; or, if not exactly a mouth, then something even better to whistle with, and if not exactly a foot, then something even better to tap with. As Frederick Buechner writes, the fact that we are resurrected *as bodies* means that God brings us back to life with everything we need to express our personalities, those things that made us who we were: the way we walked, the sound of our voices, even our faces. We shall have faces.[51]

Going back to the two faces I saw on the newsstand one morning. The Time article on keeping us forever young is based on a faith in technology and humanity's indomitable spirit. The doctrine of the resurrection of the body, on the other hand, is centered around what God does.[52] Learning how to die means trusting God with whatever it is that happens to us when that moment comes.

Jesus said, "I am the resurrection and the life." And just as God raised Jesus from the dead, the promise is that God will one

---

[51] Buechner, 51.

[52] Paraphrased from Buechner, 51-52.

day do us the same favor, breathing new life into the dust. We are living in the in-between times that come after Easter and before our own resurrection morning.

Somewhere in rural Louisiana, underneath towering oak trees, there is a woman's grave. Above the grave there is a tombstone with only a seven-letter inscription carved on it. Those seven letters are W-A-I-T-I-N-G.[53]

Waiting.

---

[53] This story is told by Philip Yancey in *The Jesus I Never Knew* (Grand Rapids, Michigan: Zondervan Publishing House, 1995), 275.

www.ingramcontent.com/pod-product-compliance
Lightning Source LLC
Chambersburg PA
CBHW052151110526
44591CB00012B/1934